Praise for *The Grateful Life*

"With inspiring stories and practical tips, *The Grateful Life* reminds us that gratitude is as much a part of a healthy lifestyle as diet and exercise. Practicing gratitude is like taking your vitamins—you don't just take them when you're sick; you also have to take them to stay healthy."

—Janine Kovac,
former editor of the *Community Gratitude Journal*
for the Greater Good Science Center

"The most magnetic trait of all time is gratitude! Want to transform your outlook and your life? Read and enjoy *The Grateful Life*."

—David Horsager, M.A., C.S.P.,
author of *The Trust Edge: How Top Leaders Gain
Faster Results, Deeper Relationships,
and a Stronger Bottom Line*

"Gratitude moves from idea to implementation. Substance pairs with serendipity in this practical and inspiring guide."

—Mary Anne Radmacher,
author of *SHE* and *Live Boldly*

Praise for the bestselling *Living Life as a Thank You*

"I have learned that the greatest joy and happiness comes from what we do to enrich other people's lives and our own spiritual lives. *Living Life as a Thank You* shows you how to connect with other people from a place of thankfulness, which in turn promotes greater harmony for all."

—Marla Maples,
actress, television host and spiritual motivator

"Twenty years ago, we gathered friends together to write about, talk about, and do Random Acts of Kindness, and from this small group, a kindness movement was born that circled the globe... With *Living Life as a Thank You*, Nina and Mary Beth have tapped into something just as deep and powerful that can truly transform people's lives."

—Will Glennon,
author of *Practice Random Acts of Kindness*

"I am grateful for the inspiring stories, the simple, clear exercises, and the inspiring reminder that an attitude of gratitude boosts self-esteem... This is a must read for everyone."

—Susyn Reeve, author of *Choose Peace & Happiness*

THE
grateful
life

THE

grateful
life

The Secret to Happiness and the
Science of Contentment

By Nina Lesowitz and Mary Beth Sammons

viva
EDITIONS

Published in the United States by Viva Editions, an imprint of Cleis Press, Inc., 2246 Sixth Street, Berkeley, California 94710.

Printed in the United States.
Cover design: Scott Idleman/Blink
Cover photograph: Fry Design Ltd./Getty Images
Text design: Frank Wiedemann

First Edition.
10 9 8 7 6 5 4 3 2 1

Trade paper ISBN: 978-1-936740-89-5
E-book ISBN: 978-1-63228-000-8

Library of Congress Cataloging-in-Publication Data

Lesowitz, Nina.
 The grateful life : the secret to happiness, and the science of contentment / Nina Lesowitz, Mary Beth Sammons. -- First edition.
    pages cm
  Includes bibliographical references and index.
 ISBN 978-1-936740-89-5 (paperback) -- ISBN 978-1-63228-000-8 (ebk)
 1. Gratitude. 2. Self-actualization (Psychology) I. Sammons, Mary Beth. II. Title.
 BF575.G68L466 2014
 179'.9--dc23
                                        2014007103

To my little grandchildren, Rylee and Tommy
—Mary Beth Sammons

To the captain of the S/V Gratitude,
Martin Eggenberger
—Nina Lesowitz

TABLE OF CONTENTS

INTRODUCTION

*We are only said to be alive in those moments
when our hearts are conscious of our treasures.*

—Thornton Wilder

What if, upon resting your head on your pillow tonight, you asked yourself, "What is one thing I can't stop smiling about that happened today?" What if you woke up to a text on your iPhone from your boss thanking you with a big "Wow, that was great" for the work you did the day before? Or what if you were having a really crummy day, running late and trying to hail a cab, and the stranger in the taxi line ahead of you said, "Here, I'm not in a hurry, you take this cab." Or what if the clerk at the coffee shop handed you your regular skim latte saying, "It's on the house—we appreciate seeing you every morning."

Gratitude is like a beacon. Whenever and wherever someone takes the time to say they are grateful for who we are and what we do, or when we pause, sometimes in the middle of really cruddy circumstances, to say thanks for the blessings we have right now, it is a powerful form of grace. As author Anne Lamott says: "Life is a phenomenon. To have been born is a miracle. What are the odds? And to just go, 'Wow, I don't get it, but thank you. Thank you.' "

If you're looking to create abundance in your life, we've got one suggestion: Be thankful, find the blessings, and practice feeling and expressing your gratitude for what you have right now, this very minute. The secret we've discovered: All things are possible when you develop an attitude of gratitude. Even in the darkest moments—you've been downsized, a flood has destroyed your home and all your belongings, doctors have just dealt you the C-word, a relative or close friend betrayed or used you—that is the time you need to stop and say, "Thank you, thank you for the strength, the courage it will take, the resilience, the change I am hoping for, and for the blessings that will help me come out the other side," because, as hard as this trial or lesson is, you promise yourself to look for the small moments, the simple solutions, and notice the blessings that continue to surround you even in the toughest times.

The Grateful Life is the third in a trilogy that started with the bestselling book *Living Life as a Thank You*, a guide to setting the stage for transformation. We moved on to *What Would You Do If You Knew You Could Not Fail?*, about overcoming fears and obstacles. Finally, this book is about discovering—and realizing—one's dreams though a positive attitude.

In 2009, we wrote *Living Life as a Thank You: The Transformative Power of Daily Gratitude*. At the time, the worst recession in decades was just swooping in, and chaos has seemed to erupt everywhere during the years that have followed: Sandy Hook Elementary School, the Boston Marathon bombings, Hurricane Sandy, Typhoon Haiyan. What is the world doing? Where is the meaning in suffering and insecurity? How, or why, should anyone be grateful?

In our interviews and research, we have discovered that a consistent practice of gratitude is the most effective way to connect to a sense of meaning. We offer stories here of resilience, reinvention, generosity, and joy, bookended by recent scientific studies that empirically prove gratitude can open the door to better health, well being, and abundance.

We include tips and inspiration from people of all races and religions who have tapped into a deeper spiritual experience and their ability to be grateful, to find blessings and meaning in the small moments, and to share the beauty that is all around, even in the most difficult and challenging of times. In embracing their gratitude, in holding their blessings like candles, they have found a way to heal their wounds. And for those who have not faced hardship, but feel a sense of disconnection or meaninglessness in their lives, these stories show how the only way to cultivate contentment is through gratitude.

Are we in the middle of a gratitude movement? Evidence suggests so, from comedian and late-night talk show host Jimmy Fallon and his hugely popular Thank You Notes, to the growing ranks of scientists who are studying how the feelings of gratitude improve physical health and emotional well-being, to people peppering their conversations and Tweets with "gratitude" or "gratefulness."

Bookstore shelves, the blogosphere, and Pinterest are filled with odes to this powerful antidote to life's challenges. Academic researchers, as well as mental health professionals, spiritual leaders, and others are also weighing in on the power of gratitude, pointing to scientific evidence showing that people who are more grateful tend to be happier, less isolated, less stressed, less depressed, and more satisfied with their lives, and to act with more generosity and compassion for others. Throughout this book, we've included the findings of scientists affiliated with the Greater Good Science Center at the University of California, Berkeley, the epicenter for research on happiness and gratitude, as well as descriptions of important studies that are taking place at Harvard University and other institutions right now.

Through years of personal practice, we have discovered that the simple act of saying "thank you" has provided us with greater fulfillment and meaning. This book contains inspiring stories from those who have used gratitude as a spiritual practice to rise out of adversity to new life, and it also shows how grateful living is central to the good life.

These stories underscore what scientists, spiritual leaders, and ordinary people leading extraordinary lives filled with gratefulness already know: Gratitude does not just happen. We are connected to others and to the power of gratefulness through a continuous acknowledgment of what we have going for us, in our lives, right now.

With gratitude,
Nina and Mary Beth

CHAPTER ONE

HOW GRATITUDE AND INTENTIONAL BEHAVIOR MOVE TO OUR HEARTS, CREATING BLESSINGS IN OUR LIVES

Man often becomes what he believes himself to be. If I keep on saying to myself that I cannot do a certain thing, it is possible that I may end by really becoming incapable of doing it. On the contrary, if I have the belief that I can do it, I shall surely acquire the capacity to do it even if I may not have it at the beginning.

—*Mahatma Gandhi*

The expression "the pursuit of happiness" implies that one has to look for—and chase after—that elusive condition labeled happiness. But somehow it always manages to stay just one step ahead. If only you could get a better job, make more money, lose weight, why, THEN you would be able to take more vacations, feel better and look better. Right? How about those "Whys?" that get in the way? "Why wasn't I born lucky?" "Why did I contract this illness?" "Why did my co-worker get the promotion that I rightly deserved?" and so on, encompassing the entirety

1

of human experiences. No, the cards are not always dealt fairly in life. But perhaps it is the act of asking those questions that is the true problem.

There are so many people (some of them profiled in this book!) who have overcome unfathomable hardships to achieve their dreams, cultivate contentment, and discover the meaning of happiness. Here's a tip: Whatever your goal may be, nothing happens until you take action. Fantasizing about change, or hoping things will fall into place perfectly for us, is natural. However, it can keep us from taking the steps necessary to transform our outlook.

When you change your focus from what you think you need in order to be happy, and instead give thanks for what you already have, you will have unlocked the process that brings about an abundant and meaningful life. Thinking grateful thoughts rewires your brain and opens up pathways that allow you to take the steps necessary to fulfill your dreams.

Bronnie Ware, a former palliative nurse in Australia, wrote a blog post that was widely received around the world. In it, she recounts the five greatest regrets of the dying.

" 'I wished I had the courage to live a life true to myself, not the life others expected of me' was the most common regret of all," she wrote. "When people realize that their life is almost over and look back clearly on it, it is easy to see how many dreams have gone unfulfilled. Most people had not honored even half of their dreams and had to die knowing that it was due to choices they had made, or not made."

If you are going to keep focusing on "Why?," "What if?" and "Why me?," which so many of us fall prey to, then one day you may regret it. However, if you take action now, and open your heart to thankfulness, you may avoid that fate and attain true, lasting happiness.

IN THE MIDST OF GRIEF:
FINDING GRATITUDE THROUGH PLAY

The best way to express our gratitude for life is by being fully alive, not hiding from life in a corner, or watching life pass us by. The biggest fear we have is not the fear of dying, but the fear to be alive, to be ourselves, to say what we feel, to ask for what we want, to say yes when we want to say yes, and no when we want to say no. To express what is in our hearts is to be truly alive. If we pretend to be what we are not, how can we be truly alive?

—Don Miguel Ruiz

MARY BETH'S STORY

A life spent camping out at a hospital bedside, holding your elderly parent's hand and your worries and stress for their illness in your heart and gut, can take a toll.

I know firsthand. During the last six years, I lived on call 24/7. It started with racing to the ER after emergency calls about my father, then my mother's heart surgery and remarkable recovery, and a year later, suddenly and swiftly, her serious illness.

The fall of 2012 was the culmination of months of doctors' appointments, followed by four months of showing up daily at my mother's hospital bedside for the new punch of bad news from the latest battery of tests. It was a rigid and heartbreaking existence. It's hard to keep smiling and joyful when you're learning each day to let go. You wake up thinking the new test will nail what's going on, but daily you feel like you are tethered to a rope that is fraying fast from a slippery slope.

In the end, after four months in two hospitals, the diagnosis: the serial killer cancer had stalked my mom as a target and won. In the dark GI lab at Loyola Medical Center, the doctor pulled me into "the room / closet" to tell me Mom had months to live, if that. The cancer was untreatable.

Where do you find gratefulness in that?

As someone who has spent a chunk of life in recent years immersed personally and professionally in the world of caregiving, I know there are volumes of books about how to care for yourself before the bubbling inferno of stress buys you a hospital bed too. I've written one and read most of them. But looking back now at the experience, as raw as it still is, I discovered what pulled me through, beyond my passionate commitment and deep-felt desire to be at both my parents' sides helping them live to the end.

Play!

Play opened the path from brokenness to the search for light in every corner of every moment I was experi-

encing. It helped me tap into a new level of consciousness. Play unplugged my fear, letting me shed tears of sorrow and joy, and gave me hope and reverence for the precious moments spent at my parent's sides.

Let me be up-front and reveal that I didn't discover play purposefully. It actually happened by accident. But it turns out that play opens the door to bliss and to gratefulness. According to Kathy Sprinkle, founder of BlissHabits.com, adventure and play are one of the 13 habits to uncover what you are grateful for and thus turn up your bliss. Here is how I tapped into the power of play to discover what I am most grateful for during a sad time marked by leavings and letting go.

At heart, I'm a preschooler, and I was lucky to have a pint-sized companion at my side: my granddaughter, Rylee, who just turned 3. In the middle of this world of caring for my parents toward the ends of their lives, Rylee's parents lived with me before and for a short while after her birth. How wonderful it was that the empty nest I was preparing for as my youngest left for college never came to fruition. It is hard to imagine my life before Rylee and the joy she brought during a challenging time.

For the last three years, during the chaos and challenges of my parents' health crises, I sneaked time to play, taking Rylee to weekly story time at Barnes & Noble and on multiple treks to the dolphin show at the Shedd

Aquarium, splashing in the fountains at the Chicago Botanic Garden, picnicking at the park, and, as the wind chill hovered in the single digits in Chicago, ice skating—our new adventure.

In the middle of being surprised by dolphins jumping and spinning in the air, of tossing my shoes and running barefoot in the garden fountain, and of sitting cross-legged listening to the story-time "teacher" share the latest antics of *Fancy Nancy*, a part of me lost in the sorrow and worry disappeared. In its place, I rediscovered the joy that play opens in our lives. Suddenly, I could see all of what was going on—caring for and loving both my parents as they lived their last moments, and spending time filled with the pure wonder of a toddler, opened me up to a gratefulness I had never known before.

Play shifted my lens. It filled me with memories of my childhood and spending times just like this with both my parents, who introduced me to the sheer pleasure of holding a good book and entering a new world through its pages. I was grateful for parents who let me gather my friends and build a tree house in our backyard. It became a childhood home-away-from-home sanctuary for the 60 kids under 12 on our block. I remembered with thankfulness my mom driving me and my friends to the skating rink, where most winters we practically lived all day, racing around the track and sipping hot chocolate.

I discovered, as Melody Beattie says, how play and gratitude unlock the fullness of life. "It turns what we have into enough, and more," she says. "It turns denial into acceptance, chaos to order, confusion to clarity. It can turn a meal into a feast, a house into a home, a stranger into a friend. Gratitude makes sense of our past, brings peace for today, and creates a vision for tomorrow."

Through play, I could let go with love of the fact that my parents would no longer physically be a part of my life. But I learned that they would live on in the books they had taught me to love, in the spirit of playfulness, and in the joy that Rylee would bring to my life as I watched her discover herself and her creativity through play.

And guess what. Apparently these opportunities to be playful are just what the doctors ordered. When it comes to stress, more giggles and playfulness are the antidote, according to Stuart Brown, founder of the National Institute for Play.

Play can't take away the stress or worry about a loved one, but data is mounting about the positive things it can do.

"Play is particularly important during periods that are sustainably stressful," writes Brown, who also is the author of *Play: How It Shapes the Brain, Opens the Imagination and Invigorates the Soul* (Penguin). Based in Carmel, California, Brown's nonprofit institute compiles research on play and provides speakers to discuss the importance of play with educational organizations and Fortune 500 companies.

Now, as my caregiving duties have transitioned to trying to gently care for the physical possessions of my parents and spending time on the phone on hold with life insurance companies, banks, and others to try to finalize what is final, I look back with greater understanding of how these small escapes were so vital.

I opened one of the boxes of my mom's belongings yesterday to discover the folder filled with photos of Rylee my sister had printed out so she would be able to stay in touch with her great-granddaughter (the wonders of Facebook). Many of them are glimpses of these adventures.

Joy and gratefulness again, in the middle of a challenging task.

GRATEFUL LIFE PRACTICE

Find a way to add play into your life every day:

- Take a walk in the woods with your dogs.
- Make a trek to the park with a pint-sized pal, or hit the swings by yourself and tap into the joy within the child inside.
- Head for the beach and splash in the waves.
- Grab your ice skates and find a skating rink.
- Pull out the Scrabble board, or construct a puzzle.
- Register for a Zumba or dance class.

THE NETWORK FOR GRATEFUL LIVING

Philosophers as far back as the ancient Greeks and Romans cited gratitude as an indispensable human virtue, but social scientists and spiritual practitioners are just beginning to study how it develops and the effects it can have.

Brother David Steindl-Rast, a Benedictine monk, is considered the spiritual leader of the gratitude movement. Author of *Gratefulness, the Heart of Prayer* (Paulist Press) and *A Listening Heart* (Crossroad/Herder), he is also the founder of www.gratefulness.org. There, The Network for Grateful Living provides education and support for the practice of grateful living as a global ethic, inspired by Br. Steindl-Rast and his colleagues' teaching.

The network maintains that gratefulness is "the full response to a given moment and all it contains." It is "a universal practice that fosters personal transformation, cross-cultural understanding, interfaith dialogue, inter-generational respect, nonviolent conflict resolution, and ecological sustainability."

IT'S MY BIRTHDAY, AND I CAN GIVE IF I WANT TO: HOW ONE WOMAN TURNED HER ANNUAL BASH INTO LIFE-ALTERING HOPE FOR ABANDONED BABIES AND CHILDREN

The Buddha taught that anyone who experiences the delight of being truly generous will never want to eat another meal without sharing it.

—Martha Beck

What did you do on your birthday? Did you dine with family and friends and bask in mutual affection and appreciation? Add 100 orphaned or abandoned young children to the mix, and that pretty much describes how Cristina Peczon, 43, has spent her birthday for almost 20 years. Cristina began feeding these infants, toddlers, and preschoolers at the White Cross Children's home in San Juan, Metro Manila, Philippines, on August 17, 1994. Although she now resides in the Southern California city of Mission Viejo with her husband and two young children, the tradition continues.

A former news anchor, broadcast journalist, and talk show host for the Philippines' leading TV network, GMA 7, and the government TV station RPN9, Cristina stated, "As you can imagine, living with your eyes glued to the screen in a Third World country isn't always a pretty picture." In this developing country, thousands of children grow up in orphanages, as their destitute parents simply cannot afford to care for them.

Incredibly, of the approximately 34 million children under the age of 18 in the Philippines, more than 2 million are orphans. And Super Typhoon Haiyan—the most devastating typhoon known to humankind, which crashed ashore on November 8, 2013, killing more than 6,000 people and leaving more than 4 million homeless—added more displaced and bereaved children to those numbers.

Since its founding in 1937, White Cross has provided temporary shelter for almost 7,000 children from newborn to age six. According to their website, 263 children have been adopted and are now living in countries around the world. For the majority who don't find "forever homes," the donations of time and money from volunteers and benefactors are often lifesaving, since White Cross does not receive any government aid or foreign funding.

Typically, orphanages are understaffed and depend on volunteers to supplement the attention and affection crucial to these children's social, physical, and emotional development. For Cristina, knowing that she is helping in some small way is the best birthday gift of all. Here is her story.

"One summer, just a week before my birthday, my boyfriend of three years broke up with me. I was crushed. In my mid-20s, I thought that he was 'the one,' " she explains. "I moped for days, more so because my birthday was coming up. In my head, it just couldn't get any worse. I went to church, got on my knees, and prayed for inspiration. On my way home to my San Juan apartment, I passed right outside the White Cross Children's Home."

As a teenager who was born and raised in the United States, Cristina had little exposure to what life was like in the Philippines. After they moved to Manila, Cristina's father took her to the White Cross orphanage during one of his company's outreach programs to show her what life was like for the less fortunate. When she was growing up, the Peczon family had a small pharmacy that was their bread and butter. If someone knocked on their door in the middle of the night because a child had a fever, Cristina's grandmother gave them medicine even if they didn't have money to pay for it.

Passing the orphanage was a sign, Cristina says: "Together with some of my closest girlfriends, we decided to visit the orphans on my birthday instead of going out to dinner. We went from room to room in the facility and spent time with the children, who offered big, warm hugs and loving smiles.

"I remember thinking, if these children, who have no idea what the future holds, could be so optimistic and cheerful, how could we complain about where we were in our lives?" she says. "It was the beginning of a love story with White Cross that has filled me with gratitude and changed my life."

The following year, on her 25th birthday, she asked all her friends and family to celebrate with her, and they brought along balloons, goody bags, and cake. They played games, and every single child won a prize. Instead of giving Cristina birthday gifts, at her request her friends brought gifts for the children. She exclaims, "It was MAGICAL! The orphans 'adopted' my friends, and they talked and shared stories, and we all fell in love."

While working in TV and living in Manila, Cristina saw firsthand how, without the intervention of White Cross, these children would likely have ended up on the streets as beggars. "The orphanage gives them all an education, a proper and loving environment to grow up in, and cares for all their needs," she says. "You can only imagine what happens to a street urchin when they become sick. At White Cross, at least there is hope that all their medical needs will be addressed with the help from generous souls who hear and offer aid."

Even with limited resources, the facility helped assist the survivors of the typhoon by sending care packages and clothes and what little they could spare for the victims in

Tacloban. "The devastation of the storm was one where everyone and anyone who had anything at all to share dug deep into their resources to do so," says Cristina. "It's just something that Filipinos do. In fact, there is a Filipino term, 'Bayanihan,' where neighbors help others to move homes when needed. It also loosely refers to the spirit of Filipinos where they help each other out when the chips are down."

In addition to celebrating her birthday at White Cross every year, sometimes Cristina would visit and play with the children. Once in a while they would ask her if that woman they saw on TV was her; she would say it was her sister, and the children would laugh and say they must be twins. "It didn't really matter to them," she says. "All that mattered was that there was someone to play with, answer silly questions, and hold hands like all little kids do. White Cross became my second home."

Every year Cristina's parties get bigger. Sometimes her friends bring their children, and friends bring more friends. One year she took the kids to the local children's museum, another year to the fair. Another year PAWS (Philippine Animal Welfare Society) came and brought their "orphaned" pets to meet the orphans. They also took the kids on outings to the local arcade, to the zoo, and to a butterfly park.

When Cristina moved back to California, the birthday party tradition continued. Her friends and family who live there still help her raise funds for the party and celebrate whether she's there or not. She also sends them packages of diapers and clothes on a regular basis.

"I am so grateful for the gifts I've received from sharing without expecting anything in return," she says. "My grandmother raised her children that way, and in turn, my parents have taught that to us.

"When we were little, I remember never being able to leave my grandmother's house without her at least offering to give me something to bring home. Or maybe she had picked up one of my favorites that she saw at the store when she knew I was coming to visit. She was always sharing and giving. She died at the ripe old age of 107 with a smile on her face…, and I believe it was because she was a happy giver. That's what made her happy."

The tradition of giving is being passed along to the next generation.

"My friends who have taken their children to the orphanage say that, when they go home, their children start to say things like, 'Maybe I don't need to have new shoes since the orphans have nothing' or 'Can we send things to the orphans this year instead of buying new things for us?' "

Cristina says that many times people want to help and share, but they just don't know how or where to channel their efforts. "There was one year of terrible storms where the children would try to crawl out of their cribs when the thunder scared them at night," she says. "So I contacted all my friends and asked them to help me raise funds to have special low cribs built for the children. Another year we raised funding to replace the old and rotten flooring in one of the dormitories. Short on funds, we used what we had to buy all the odds and ends from a local tile distributor—and with the tiles we bought we created a gorgeous mosaic pattern on the dormitory floor. That room eventually was given a citation from the department of social welfare and development for its innovation in uplifting orphanage life in the Philippines."

She is also contacted by strangers who ask how they can throw parties for the White Cross and similar charity organizations. Many of them are tourists who plan on visiting the orphanage as part of their adventure to the Philippines. Cristina's friend Karen Kunawicz, who attended all the White Cross parties, has been inspired to help another charity, the children of the Philippine General Hospital, which is usually where the poorest of the poor go for medical help, according to Cristina. To learn more about the work that Cristina does at White Cross, you can go to www.facebook.com/christina.peczonrodriguez or inolongernewswatch.wordpress.com.

GRATEFUL LIFE PRACTICE
Have you ever been intrigued by the concept of a volunteer vacation? Are you the type who gets bored sitting on a

beach towel all day? According to International Volunteers Program Association (IVPA), there are countless reasons why thousands of people volunteer abroad each year. You may start with a desire to travel, learn a new language, or meet new people. By volunteering, you'll also have the opportunity to lend a hand to those who are working to improve life in their communities. Through your daily work and interactions with members of a local community, you'll gain a better understanding of the culture, as well as of the issues that affect that part of the world. You'll also learn a lot about yourself, as you take on the challenge of living and working in a completely new environment. The IVPA website, www.volunteerinternational.org, offers very detailed information, and we recommend that you start by going to the tab "Selecting the Right Program."

There are many programs, and, if you decide you really want to do this, you will want to do extensive research before you select the one for you. Another resource that allows you to review a variety of opportunities that are either free or low-cost is www.vaops.com.

There is also a book, *Volunteer Vacations: Short-Term Adventures That Will Benefit You and Others*, by Bill McMillon, Doug Cutchins, and Anne Geissinger, with a foreword by Ed Asner, currently in its 11th edition, that may inspire you to dedicate your next vacation to helping others. Happy travels!

SWEET BLESSINGS:
MEANINGFUL COINCIDENCES CARRY
ON HER PARENTS' FULLNESS OF LIFE

*When we lose one blessing, another is often most
unexpectedly given in its place.*

—C.S. Lewis

*It has been 25 years since Mary Amore's mother passed
away from lung cancer. Yet Mary remembers the day as
if it were yesterday: the heaviness and loss that engulfed
her. Along with her best friend and her three-year-
old daughter, Lauren, she would spend precious days
window-shopping at the beautifully landscaped Oak
Brook Shopping Center near her home. There they'd sit
by the fountains, watching the toddler play and soaking
in conversations, hot cups of coffee, and Mrs. Field's
chocolate chip cookies.*

Cancer had swept in and stolen Mary's rock. The

memories surfaced amid the anguish and emptiness as Mary waited outside her mother's room at Loyola Medical Center, after doctors told her that her mom's time on earth was coming to an end. Having been raised a strict Catholic in the pre-Vatican II era, she flashed back and suddenly felt haunted by what nuns at her school told her when she was only eight years old: "Your mother is going to go to hell when she dies." Mary's mom, it turns out, was Lutheran, which was why the school sisters had said her mother's soul would burn in eternity. Fortunately, Mary's mom understood the fear in her little daughter's eyes, and reassured Mary that they would certainly be together in heaven one day. Mary had never given this topic much thought until this night.

Mary remembers feeling desperate, fearing for her mother's soul, and so when a priest arrived at the hospital and asked her what he could do for her mom, she pleaded, "Please make her Catholic." The priest just looked at Mary. Then he said, "Wait here." He went into her mother's hospital room. Minutes later he returned to Mary and reassured her that "it's all taken care of." A huge weight was lifted from Mary. Ten hours later, her mom passed, and Mary was at peace.

On that evening, Mary says she learned something important about life and humanity. For all the grief and agony the nuns caused her worrying about her mother's soul in the afterlife, the priest had been present for Mary and taken care of her by fulfilling this final wish for her mom. He didn't balk, or insist the family bring in a religious tribunal, or forbid her mother's baptism based on canon law; he simply moved in to bring peace and grace to a mother and her grown-up daughter during her final hours of life.

No one can truly understand or know the depth of what is taken away from you when a loved one dies or how one finds peace in grief and loss. But for Mary that experience became the first in a lifetime of blessings that have been ushered into her life following the passing of her mother and, a year later, her father. She says they come wrapped in what she calls "candy kisses," providential happenings or meaningful coincidences that connect her directly to their souls and to the fullness of life they had envisioned for their daughter and her family. The "candy kisses" connect her to God.

As a young girl, Mary Amore had one dream—to travel the world or, greater yet, the universe. Growing up in the 1960s, she considered various careers: travel agent, flight attendant, astronaut, or perhaps even joining the Rockettes. The only problem was that she was terrified of heights, ruling out a career in the friendly skies and jet-setting to exotic locales. The Big Apple and her name in lights wouldn't work either; she was too short. "I figured, I just have to plan travel from the ground."

Fast-forward: Mary met the man of her dreams and set up house in Downer's Grove, Illinois, and became a mother to her daughter, Lauren, and four years later her son, Joey. Life was good.

But then, in February 1989, while her father was being treated for a broken hip, her mother was rushed to the ER when the lung cancer she had been battling reared its ugly head, and Mary found herself on that lonely night holding vigil during her mom's end of life.

Shortly after her mother passed away, Mary's physician encouraged her to have a routine baseline mammogram. She thought it was pointless—after all, she was only 39 at the time—but she got the test and left on a vacation. She returned to discover that it was now her turn: She was facing the reality of breast cancer.

Having just experienced cancer with her mom, Mary was frozen in fear. The one thing she did know for certain, after her mother's death at a relatively young age, was that she would do what it took to fight for her life. She decided to have a prophylactic mastectomy.

Her prayer mantra throughout the entire decision-making process was, "Lord, help me to know that this is the right decision for me." She prayed this incessantly.

Then came the first "candy kiss" / blessing. On hearing her decision about a prophylactic mastectomy, her surgeon said, "Mary, this is the right decision for you."

"My exact prayer mantra had just been spoken through

my surgeon," she remembers. "At that moment, a feeling of peace and tranquility washed over me, and I truly felt God's presence holding me. I knew somehow I would be all right." There was a special song that she would listen to in memory of her mom: "The Wind beneath My Wings." Her mom had never heard it because it was released after she was gone, but nonetheless Mary called it *their song.*

On the morning of her mastectomy, as she was wheeled into surgery, Mary heard the gentle strains of "The Wind beneath My Wings" playing over the sound system. "I knew my mom was right there with me at that moment," she says. "I really felt her heavenly presence, and I was not afraid. God sent my mother to comfort me in my darkest hour."

Mary had come to discover that she would always be connected to her mother and father; in fact, they were continuing to communicate with her in meaningful and often very powerful ways. Psychologist Carl Jung had a theory about such "signs" or "meaningful coincidences" (conjunctions of events that seem imbued with mystical significance). He believed that, in addition to the usual cause-and-effect relationship of events, there was "a causal connecting principle." He termed this synchronicity.

Jung certainly described Mary's experienced to a T.

A year after her mother passed, on New Year's Eve, Mary and her husband, Joe, were both suffering from stomach flu when they got a call from the hospital's ER and were told to come fast: "Your dad is not going to make it." Mary remembers saying it wasn't a good idea for her to be bringing the flu germs into the hospital, but the doctor told her: "Did you hear what I said? Your dad is not going to make it through the night." So she raced over and said goodbye to her father, who was breathing with great difficulty. She waited by his bedside until she could no longer stand. Then she returned home awaiting news.

The next day, her birthday, she returned to the hospital, not knowing what to expect. She remembers passing the nurse's station and seeing a sign overhead that read, "Expect a miracle." She found her dad, who had received what had been described as a visit from the Angel of Death, sitting up in a chair, eating prime rib. She, her husband, and her dad had a wonderful day swapping memories and soaking in the seemingly miraculous turn of events. When they were leaving the hospital, Mary instructed her husband to look at the sign over the nurse's station. Only thing was, when they looked up, the sign that had so clearly sent her a powerful message that morning was no longer there. Another "candy kiss."

"I look back, and I know that my dad, who was in his last days, just refused to die on my birthday," says Mary. For 14 days, she would stop at McDonald's and pick up coffee and a cheese Danish to bring to him in the hospital. But the extension didn't last for long. Her dad's heart was failing, and the doctors called her to say he could no longer stay in the hospital; he would have to be cared for in a nursing home. All her life, Mary had promised her parents that she would not put them in a nursing home. Now she had to tell her dad otherwise.

In the short drive to the hospital, Mary asked God to take her dad home, and to let her be there when he passed from this life to the next. She knew he had given up, and just wanted to go "home to heaven." That morning they watched *Casablanca* together and had a wonderful father-daughter visit. However, Mary still hadn't found the courage to tell her dad that the next day he would be put into a nursing home. She told him she would go home and come back later for another visit. As she was putting on her coat to leave, her dad's heart just stopped, and he passed away in her presence. Mary knew her prayers were answered, and even in this grief-filled moment, she was at peace.

"I felt very blessed that I had 36 wonderful years with my parents," says Mary. "I learned that, even in the midst of what seems like great loss and tragedy, God is always with us and the blessings are always there."

These days, the "candy kisses" keep coming. Before Mary and her family left on a recent trip to Italy, she stood at her mom's graveside and said, "Mom, I wish you could come with us." When their plane landed in Italy, a sign at the airport said, "Alice welcomes you to Rome." Alice is her mom's name.

Oh—about the travel agent plans. Turns out God had a different kind of travel adventure in story for Mary. Shortly after her two children started elementary school, God called Mary out of the kitchen and into ministry, where she earned a master of arts degree in pastoral studies and a doctor of ministry in liturgy from the Catholic Theological Union in Chicago. A Cardinal Bernardin Scholar and a distinguished member of the North American Academy of Liturgy, these days she is Dr. Mary Amore, Executive Director of Mayslake Ministries, a spiritual "retreat house without walls" in Downers Grove, Illinois.

GRATEFUL LIFE PRACTICE
A devotion to daily prayer is how Mary practices gratitude each day. Her advice is to look for four messages—in scripture passages and inspirational quotes—to write down and serve up as "soul snacks" to keep you in touch with the source of gratefulness in each day. She says: "The minute I am aware of a 'candy kiss' moment unfolding, or a moment of divine inspiration or help, I immediately thank God over and over again in my mind and heart. I usually try and focus on a picture of Jesus as I am doing my thanks…, but, either way, I stop everything, and it is an instantaneous moment of heartfelt gratitude and thanksgiving. Simple but powerful."

GRATITUDE PRAYER

Be Thankful
Be thankful that you don't already have everything you
    desire,
If you did, what would there be to look forward to?
Be thankful when you don't know something
For it gives you the opportunity to learn.
Be thankful for the difficult times.
During those times you grow.
Be thankful for your limitations
Because they give you opportunities for improvement.
Be thankful for each new challenge
Because it will build your strength and character.
Be thankful for your mistakes
They will teach you valuable lessons.
Be thankful when you're tired and weary
Because it means you've made a difference.
It is easy to be thankful for the good things.
A life of rich fulfillment comes to those who are

also thankful for the setbacks.
GRATITUDE can turn a negative into a positive.
Find a way to be thankful for your troubles
and they can become your blessings.

—*Author Unknown*

CHAPTER TWO
LIVING LIFE WITH PASSION: HOW GRATITUDE CAN CLARIFY YOUR LIFE PURPOSE

Reflect upon your present blessings—of which every man has many—not on your past misfortunes, of which all men have some.

—Charles Dickens

Through our research and writing, we have seen how harnessing the power of gratitude can lead to a discovery of our life purpose, which in turn leads to a greater sense of self-worth. A more appreciative mind-set can help shift our thoughts from negative ones, which cycle in a vicious loop, to positive ones, which open up pathways to possibility.

For instance, this chapter includes a story about a world-champion golfer, a young man in his 20s, who chose not to focus on his sudden loss of vision while attending college, but instead on the blessings in his life. This young man could have easily fallen into a morass of self-pity, which would have sunk him even further. Instead, by focusing on the positive, he was able to realize his dream vocation: giving inspirational speeches and competing in golf tournaments.

There are many books and articles that center on "finding your purpose." Don't despair if that concept seems elusive. For many, it's a process that slowly unfolds over time. It doesn't necessarily need to come to you in one single "light bulb moment," although it may.

For most, it's a journey that includes an acceptance of self, a willingness to open up to new experiences and beliefs, and a commitment to appreciating the here and now instead of focusing only on the future. As so many of the stories throughout this book illustrate, gratitude is often the key to personal fulfillment and a shortcut to a sense of abundance.

Here are a few more inspiring stories.

HE LOST HIS SIGHT AND FOUND HIS MISSION: WORLD BLIND GOLF CHAMPION HELPS OTHERS TO VISUALIZE SUCCESS

Keep your face always toward the sunshine—and shadows will fall behind you.

—Walt Whitman

Heading to class at San Diego State University one day in 2008, Jeremy Poincenot, an active sophomore, found he had trouble reading a sign on the campus. That night he needed to squint to read a textbook. Since he'd always had 20/20 vision, he assumed he simply needed glasses or contacts, but when he went to the optometrist and covered his left eye, he couldn't even read the big E on the eye chart. Over the next month he lost central vision in his other eye.

Jeremy's doctor thought it might be a brain tumor, and for weeks he was misdiagnosed with other, more common, problems that cause sudden, painless vision loss, until he eventually learned that he had Leber's Hereditary Optic Neuropathy (LHON), a rare genetic disorder that left him legally blind. He remembers that his doctor wished him good luck but did not encourage him with any pep talks. As Jeremy says, "I would have been elated if he told me about someone with LHON who persevered and became a champion like I did."

Today Jeremy is on a mission to remedy that oversight. Through his powerful story, he hopes to show others that anything is possible. Here he describes how losing his sight helped him become a stronger, more confident, and more driven individual, dedicated to helping others find their passion and turn adversity into triumph. Or in Jeremy's case, turning his "handicap" into a golf trophy.

Declaring that he is happier now than he was at 19 when he had 20/20 vision and a golf handicap of four, Jeremy Poincenot of Carlsbad, California, asserts that the loss of his sight was the catalyst for "living his dream."

That didn't happen overnight, though. "I was devastated and depressed, and I asked, 'Why me?' every day for a month. I didn't think it was possible to go legally blind so quickly at age 19, and couldn't believe there was no treatment and no cure," he says.

Jeremy woke up every morning reluctantly, because "in my dreams, I could see. When I awoke, everything was blurry." He feared his life as he knew it was over. Then one day, while watching TV, he continues, "I saw this guy who had just lost his wife, mother-in-law, and two young daughters when a plane crashed down on his house. The guy was in a press conference crying, saying 'If anybody knows how to handle something this tragic, please help me.' I just thought, 'Hey, if this guy can make it through this then I can survive having no central vision.'"

Jeremy is eternally grateful for his support system: his brother, sister, fraternity brothers, friends, and parents, who have been instrumental in helping him to find his calling. His fraternity brothers at SDSU walked him to classes and helped him get wherever he needed to go. His mother, Lissa, set up the website LHON.org to provide information to help other families affected by LHON in need of support.

His father, Lionel, a club engineer at Callaway Golf, got him back on the golf course six months after losing his sight. Blind golf is played as a team sport, and Jeremy's father helps by lining him up. Jeremy places his chin on his dad's shoulder as he's pointing, to get a sense of the correct alignment. Their partnership worked so well that in 2010 Jeremy won the World Blind Golf Championship in Britain, beating a field of 60 from 14 countries.

Jeremy has gone on to become an inspirational speaker, which he describes as his dream job, and he expresses gratitude for the fact that he now has a clear-cut identity. "At 19, I was searching for what I was going to do with my life," he says. "Now I am focused on things that are greater than me. I no longer take things for granted. It's very powerful to be able to share my story. Very cool."

He describes how gratifying it is to receive messages on his Facebook wall like the one from a LHON-challenged U.K. resident who wrote, "Seeing your optimism makes me feel like I could be happier." Jeremy's advice to others is to do what they love, and strive to get better every day. "Because I am playing at a high level internationally, it gives me a reason to keep going. I can't get bummed out; I have to stay driven."

In addition to practicing his game and speaking to audiences nationwide, Jeremy works hard to raise funds so that researchers can find a cure for his disorder. His mom, sister, and brother are at risk of blindness, which contributes to the urgency of his mission. Jeremy and his friends created C.U.R.E. (Cycling under Reduced Eyesight), an annual fund-raising bike ride that his fraternity brothers avidly participate in. Jeremy's goal is to raise $1 million to help fund research to find a cure for this rare disorder. He and his mother have also set up a LHON fund where people can donate toward the cause on the LHON.org site. Today Jeremy is fully focused on the future, and dedicated to sharing this maxim with others: Focus on what you have, rather than what you don't. In Jeremy's case, he chooses to be grateful for the peripheral sight he has retained, rather than the central vision he has lost.

GRATEFUL LIFE PRACTICE

When Jeremy was diagnosed, his mother connected with a man who lost his vision decades ago. He told her about Ski for Light, a cross-country skiing program for blind, visually impaired, and mobility impaired adults. His advice was that the most important thing she could do for Jeremy was to help him remain active and find ways to continue to participate in sports. The Challenged Athletes Foundation (CAF) provides opportunities and support to people with physical disabilities so they can pursue active lifestyles through physical fitness and competitive athletics. CAF believes that involvement in sports at any level increases self-esteem, encourages independence, and enhances quality of life. You can make a huge difference in the lives of challenged athletes by fund-raising, volunteering, supporting a local region, shopping the online store, or joining their community: www.challengedathletes.org. To find out more about Jeremy, go to his website: www. jeremypoincenot.com.

HONORING HOME AND HEARTH
WITH GRATITUDE

In 1994, Cathy Zimmerman and her husband, Fred, moved into "a very modest home in a very middle-class neighborhood" in Chicago's western suburb of Downer's Grove. The price was right, the space was very open and light, and they could walk to town.

"Having just come from living in downtown Chicago, having access to city life was of utmost importance to us," she says.

Their suburban downtown was simple: a Walgreens Pharmacy, a 100-year-old hardware store, a five-and-dime, a bagel store, and a historic though somewhat neglected railroad station. Added to that was an adorable post office and a small but wonderful library.

"I recognized at once that I was very fortunate to be in this humble village that, since 1832, so many had proudly called home," she says. "I immediately began a practice of gratitude that I have continued to this day. Every time I write my street address—return address on holiday cards, filling in forms, jotting down my address for friends— EVERY SINGLE TIME, I mindfully write down my full street address with no abbreviations. This is my home, a noble abode with a great past, present, and future, and its address deserves that extra respect and attention. This is an honorable piece of land with much integrity. Each time I write my street address in full, I bless this place and envision love, peace, and prosperity."

As the years go by, Cathy says, "My piece of heaven has evolved, and so have my surroundings." The schools turned out to be award-winning, the library was expanded and a children's section added, a fountain and landscaping were installed at the train station, and the town is now a preferred destination for many, listed by *Forbes* magazine as one of the top 10 friendliest towns in America. And Cathy and Fred's Randall Park neighborhood hosts a Turkey Bowl, Breakfast with Santa, and a Soapbox Derby, and recently sent seven full school buses of relief supplies to the victims of the Washington, Illinois, tornadoes.

"I am thankful for this place—my home—and all that it has given to me and to my family," says Cathy. "I am also grateful that, over the years and in return, my home has graciously accepted all of our love and attention. Thank you, 5401 Park Avenue, Downers Grove, Illinois 60515. I love you and am OH so very grateful."

LAUGHING YOURSELF TO HEALTH AND HEALING: HUMOR AS A TOOL TO STAY POSITIVE AND LIVE LONGER

The human race has only one really effective weapon, and that's laughter. The moment it arises, all our hardness's yield, all our irritations and resentments slip away, and a sunny spirit takes their place.

—Mark Twain

According to researchers at the Albert Einstein College of Medicine and Yeshiva University, people who are optimistic, laugh a lot, and are easygoing may live longer. That is not news to Allen Klein, a pioneer in the therapeutic humor movement and the author of 20 books ranging from The Healing Power of Humor, *published in 1989, to* Always Look on the Bright Side, *published in 2013.*

The recipient of a Lifetime Achievement Award from the Association for Applied and Therapeutic Humor, Allen discovered the restorative value of humor when his wife, Ellen, died at the age of 34 in 1978. He has since dedicated his life to helping others navigate the minefield of loss—mindfully, and sometimes mirthfully—through his speaking engagements, workshops, and books. His books alone have been published in eight different languages (English, Spanish, Danish, Japanese, Korean, Chinese, Hungarian, and Turkish) with over 600,000 in print. Klein, aka Mr. Jollytologist, knows that humor can help us deal with everyday trials and tribulations and triumph over tragedy. He credits his positive attitude for making miracles happen.

Allen Klein recently added another subject to his repertoire of talks: "Making Miracles Happen." In this talk, he describes some of the acts of serendipity that have happened to him and continue to happen to him, and then explains how others can manifest miracles in their own lives, each and every day.

A very important element, he says, is to begin by stating your intention. No matter how big or how small, or how many people tell you "it will never happen" (which is precisely what Allen was told when he voiced his desire to someday march in the Macy's Thanksgiving Day Parade), make sure you give voice to your dreams and desires. In November 2013, Allen did, in fact, march in the 87th annual parade, fulfilling one of his lifelong dreams by cavorting alongside Snoopy, the cast of Cirque de Soleil, numerous celebrities, and hundreds of other joyful participants.

Allen keeps a gratitude journal, and he states very simply: Gratitude makes one happier. He mixes gratitude with his spiritual beliefs and a sprinkling of levity, and creates a space that allows his intentions to come to fruition. It wasn't always this easy for him, though. Like so many others, Allen had to find his way through hardship and loss before he became the joyful person he is today. "It's almost more important to be grateful for the not-so-good things that happen to you," he says. "Those negative experiences taught me the most. And now I can teach others what I've learned in my journey."

A former resident of New York City, where he worked as a scenic designer at CBS-TV, Allen and his wife moved to San Francisco, where Ellen was originally from. They bought and operated a successful silk-screening business and enjoyed living in their dream Victorian house. Tragically, Ellen came down with primary biliary cirrhosis—a chronic disease that causes the bile ducts in the liver to become inflamed and damaged and, ultimately, to disappear—and died a few short years after their move cross-country.

Not long after, Allen received a brochure in the mail that coincided with his epiphany that "silk-screening was not what I was supposed to be doing." It was from the Holistic Life Institute in San Francisco. He decided to enroll in their Death and Dying course. Over time, Allen became director of that program, and also became a hospice volunteer and home health aide.

While immersed in a world of grief and emotional pain, he read about Norman Cousins, editor of the *Saturday Review* and also an adjunct professor of medical humanities for the school of medicine at the University of California, Los Angeles, where he did research on the biochemistry of human emotions. When Cousins himself was diagnosed with a very painful form of arthritis called ankylosing spondylitis and given a grim prognosis (a one in 500 chance of recovery), he decided to take matters into his own hands. One day, against the advice of his doctors, Cousins left the hospital and isolated himself in his apartment to read humorous stories and watch comedy movies. At the end of one month of daily guffawing, Cousins returned to the hospital for a checkup. He was completely cured, to the astonishment of the medical staff who examined him. His at-the-time radical views were finally vindicated in January 27, 1989, when the *Journal of the American Medical Association* published an article entitled "Laugh If This Is a Joke."

That struck a chord with Allen. Remembering humorous moments with his deceased wife were helping him to heal. Allen went on to receive his master's degree in human development and, from there, developed a three-hour workshop on the healing power of humor in which he presents a series of proven techniques for overcoming the negative effects of loss, setbacks, upsets, disappointments, trials, and tribulations. He teaches that the ability to laugh at annoyances, crises, and even outright disasters can literally save your life.

Allen also tapped into the healing power of gratitude during this time.

"After my wife died, my thoughts sometimes turned to darker questions like, 'How can I go on with my life without her?' Grief also brought up feelings of emptiness, depression, and hopelessness," he says. "Once I started to be thankful for all that remained in my life—my daughter, my friends, my work, etc.—I got a glimpse of why I could go on living and, in fact, fully enjoy life again.

"One of my spiritual teachers once told me that when we want what we don't have, we waste what we do have," Allen continues. "To translate that into loss-related situations, to want what is no longer in our life is to waste what still remains in our life." He further advises, try to laugh! Allen knows that humor is a great coping mechanism. "Finding the humor in anything and laughing about it gives you a break from the pain of loss. It also provides a breath of fresh air at a time when everything seems dark and heavy.

"Appropriate humor can help people cope. It empowers them. It is defiant, triumphant, and life-affirming," according to Allen. "It provides perspective and balance. And it diverts attention, provides comic relief, and liberates patients, families, and caregivers from their loss."

GRATEFUL LIFE PRACTICE

In Allen's book *Learning to Laugh When You Feel Like Crying*, he suggests a simple way to move towards being grateful after a loss. Tomorrow morning, before you get out of bed, think of at least one thing that you are thankful for. And then, when you get out of bed, start writing down all the wonderful things in your life. You can be thankful for:

- a coin found on the street
- the cookies a neighbor brought you
- the friends you have
- a rainbow
- flowers in the park
- a cup of tea

Those are just a few little "gratitudes" that can keep you afloat while you are in a sea of grief. But you might also want to note some of the bigger things for which you are grateful. For example:

- that the deceased was in your life
- the lessons you learned from them
- that their spirit still lives within you

And you can be grateful for life itself. As comedian Robin Williams discovered after his heart surgery, "When you have something like heart surgery, you appreciate the simple things, like breathing."

ALL THAT IS POSSIBLE: BUSY EXECUTIVE
CONNECTS TO THE HOMELESS WITH COMPASSION

*Take the first step in faith. You don't have to take
the whole staircase, just take the first step.*

—Dr. Martin Luther King Jr.

*The man sat in his wheelchair under the El tracks at Wells
and Monroe Streets in Chicago. Every morning, Vickie
Rock, a busy CEO and president of one of the largest
court-reporting firms in the city, raced by him, en route
from the train station to her office in the heart of the city's
financial district. She noticed that his left side was paralyzed, his voice crackled when the El engineer would honk
his horn, and the man would shout "Hello," and raise his
right hand in greeting.*

*Vickie never just walked by like throngs of others; she
always put coins, and sometimes gift coupons for Wendy's*

or McDonald's, into his cup. But the idea that it wasn't enough, the idea that this man spent his days on the street corner haunted her and tugged at her heart.

Then one day she walked back.

"I realized that every day going to work I would see all these homeless people on the streets and didn't know what to do, so I'd give them fast-food gift certificates or cash," she says. "But it never felt right just handing them something and walking away. I always wondered, 'What were their stories?' I was very afraid, but I made it a point that I was going to get their stories and do something."

She would learn that the man, Willie Brown, was homeless, living sometimes in an apartment on the city's South Side, paying $20 a day to stay there and another $20 to have someone carry him up the three flights of steps to the apartment.

Thus began a sweet, heartfelt connection that would carry on for almost five years. During that time, Vickie arranged to get Willie an electric wheelchair and invited him into her office to connect him with services, like making doctor's appointments or working through the Department of Aging to help him find a home. He would be the first of several homeless people whom she has helped connect to employment opportunities and food and shelter.

Many in the cynical business world who tune out the homeless as a nuisance they pass on the way to work do

*not understand the special bond Vickie feels for home-
less people or the risks she is taking doing what she does.
But for Vickie it wasn't a conscious decision to care. She
says she just knows there was a connection and a pull for
her to help. She says she thinks it is out of thankfulness
for her own life and possibly a connection she feels with
others who are vulnerable, born out of her own complicated and fragile childhood. Here is the La Grange, Illinois, woman's story.*

Vickie Rock was 10 years old when her parents got divorced.
The situation was complicated and "pretty rough" on
Vickie, her mom, and her two siblings—older sister Eileen
and younger brother Ricky. Their home in Indiana was
foreclosed on, child support payments abruptly stopped,
and they ended up moving to a two-bedroom apartment
in Blue Island, just south of Chicago. They rarely saw
their father, who had married a woman with two children
and fathered another son with his second wife. When his
second wife died, he married his caregiver.

"My dad remarried right away, and my mom worked all
the time to try to keep us afloat," she remembers. During
high school Vickie and her sister worked as waitresses at
the same coffee shop, De Mars Family Restaurant, where
her brother bussed tables and her mom worked as a hostess.
"My grandmother was a big influence in helping us, but we
were pretty isolated," Vickie says. "We had been baptized

Catholic, but we had disconnected from the church."

Her parents, she would later learn, were forced to marry at 16 when her mom got pregnant, and the relationship had spiraled into one filled with emotional and sometimes physical abuse. "I had some pretty bad abandonment issues," says Vickie. "I felt not worthy because of everything that happened in my childhood."

At 20, she married her high school sweetheart, but the union ended in a divorce within three years.

Meantime, Vickie was driven to build her career, starting as a legal secretary, then working as a court reporter and moving up the ladder to launch several of her own firms, including Victoria Court Reporting Service Inc., where she serves as CEO and president today.

But something always felt like it was missing. That is when Vickie went to a weekend program where she tried to deal with her abandonment issues. The miracle that occurred following her commitment to heal herself was setting up a time to meet with her father. "I wanted to hear his story," she says.

She sat, listened, and learned that her father's father, her paternal grandfather, had been killed in a train accident when her father was 12; his mother remarried, and his stepfather did not like kids, so they sent her father to live elsewhere. "He had major abandonment issues too," she says.

Today, she says that the forgiveness and healing she felt

was a gift, a major turning point in her life. She's now married to Rick, an attorney, and the duo live in Western Springs, a suburb west of Chicago. When she met Rick, what attracted her was his strong faith and commitment to his spiritual path.

Inspired by her reconciliation with her father and her husband's spiritual journey, Vickie is grateful for the strength and healing that have come through her strong Catholic faith, which she discovered was never fully extinguished. She is now again strongly connected to the church.

"I feel so blessed to be where I am in life, and I feel it is my responsibility to reach out to others who are hurting," she says.

Though Willie suddenly disappeared and she has never seen him again, Vickie has reached out time and time again to form unexpected and life-changing connections with others whose path she crosses on the streets of Chicago on her journey to work.

There's Marvin, an elderly black gentleman who stands in front of the drugstore at Adams and Wells Streets, who every morning greets the throngs of commuters passing by on their way to their offices in Chicago's Loop with a cheery, "Good morning, God bless you." And there was the young man, in a business suit, who stood at the train station passing out his résumé after losing his job. Vickie helped circulate the résumé after approaching him, listening to his story, and reaching out to help.

"Looking back at my life, I see it truly was a 'foot-prints in the sand,' where God was carrying me through the most difficult of times," she says. "I was born in a line of nurturing, caring, strong women. I have a greater appreciation of all my mother went through to support and raise me and my sister and brother and how difficult that must have been for her. My grandmother took in my aunt Mary at age 12, who really was a neighbor's child and had been thrown out of her home by her mentally ill mother. She also took in my Japanese cousin, Mary Kay, whose mother, KiKi, took her life when she was shunned by so many Americans when my great uncle brought her home with him after his service in World War II. And, finally, my great grandmother too, who single-handedly transported her four children from Scotland to Canada to Chicago."

Love, acts of kindness, forgiveness, keeping the Lord in focus at all times, and being in service to others is truly what Vickie's life is about.

GRATEFUL LIFE PRACTICE

Vickie holds Bible study classes for her colleagues who work in the city of Chicago to reflect on the spiritual roots of their blessings—and her daily giving to the homeless is part of her gratitude practice.

SOME STATISTICS WE CAN APPRECIATE

Charity: Grateful people give an average of 20 percent more to charities.

Psychology: Gratitude is related to age. For every 10 years, gratitude increases by 5 percent.

Community: Grateful people have a stronger bond with the community.

Health: Grateful people will have 10 percent fewer stress-related illnesses, are more physically fit, and have blood pressure that is lower by 12 percent.

Work: The incomes of grateful people are an average of 7 percent higher.

Friends: Grateful people have more satisfying relationships with others and are liked more.

School: Grateful people are 20 percent more likely to get "A" grades; 13 percent have fewer fights.

Location: The most grateful countries are South Africa, the United Arab Emirates, the Philippines, and India.

Life: Overall positive emotions can add seven years to your life.

—Reprinted from a graphic developed by
Heresmychance.com.

CHAPTER THREE

THE GRATEFUL WORKPLACE:
INCREASE PRODUCTIVITY AND HAPPINESS
WHILE YOU WORK

Appreciation can make a day, even change a life.
Your willingness to put it into words is all that is
necessary.

—Margaret Cousins

According to a survey of 2,000 Americans released in 2013 by the John Templeton Foundation, people are less likely to feel or express gratitude at work than anyplace else. And they're not thankful for their current jobs, ranking them *last* in a list of things they're grateful for.

In an article by Jeremy Adam Smith, producer and editor at the Greater Good Science Center at the University of California, Berkeley, he elaborates on the study: "Almost all respondents reported that saying 'thank you' to colleagues 'makes me feel happier and more fulfilled' "— but on a given day, only 10 percent acted on that impulse.

A stunning 60 percent said they "either never express gratitude at work or do so perhaps once a year. In short, Americans actively suppress gratitude on the job, even to the point of robbing themselves of happiness."

But the good news is that there are people who are taking on the gargantuan task of increasing happiness on the job, by studying, coaching, and counseling supervisors and employees. This not only improves businesses' bottom lines, but also affects everyone who works, or is related to someone who has a job, or shops for products or services. Seriously—if you are thanked for your business, you will more likely be a repeat customer and recommend that person, business, or organization to your friends.

In this chapter, we also see how two women—one a nurse, the other a wellness coach—came up with a wonderful idea that they spread throughout their community by convincing retailers, restaurant owners, librarians, and others that their storefront windows could become a canvas of gratitude—and that business would flourish as a result.

Another exciting development is the focus of some researchers who, instead of analyzing corporate failures, are focusing on compassion across cubicles. One such movement, called Positive Organizational Scholarship (POS), looks for examples of "positive deviance"—cases in which organizations successfully cultivate inspiration and productivity among workers. A leader in POS, Jane

Dutton, a professor of psychology and business at the University of Michigan, and her colleagues have studied hospitals, universities, and businesses like Newsweek, Reuters, Macy's, and Cisco Systems to learn how organizations respond to employees experiencing personal difficulty.

Their studies yielded some stories of compassion, where distressed workers received cards, flowers, financial help, emotional support, or time off from work; in other cases, workers complained of receiving little sympathy or help. They found that employees who'd experienced compassion at work saw themselves, their co-workers, and the organization in a more positive light. Statistics further demonstrated that this elicited more positive emotions, such as joy and contentment, and more commitment to the organization. These results held regardless of whether employees received compassion directly or merely witnessed it.

All we can say is "Hallelujah!" It's been a long time, but change is coming to the workplace, and we know it will have ripple effects that will benefit everyone.

THINKING OUTSIDE THE CORPORATE BOX: WHY APPRECIATION IN THE WORKPLACE IS LIFE CHANGING

People want to be appreciated, not impressed. They want to be regarded as human beings, not as mere sounding boards for other people's egos. They want to be treated as an end in themselves, not as a means toward the gratification of another's vanity.

—Sydney J. Harris

It all began in 2010 when Lisa Ryan and a group of her friends hopped in the car and drove five hours from Cleveland to attend a Tony Robbins motivational seminar. Over the course of four days, they walked on lighted charcoal, tapped into the power within, and drove back "on fire" with plans to transform their entire lives. The circle of friends agreed to launch their new and inspired selves by regularly posting what they were most grateful for on Facebook.

"We opened up a Facebook thread and shared three things that we were grateful for," she remembers. "We did

this every day, and we held each other accountable for contributing. I had no idea the impact that this practice would have on my life."

Shortly after launching the Facebook gratitude page, this Cleveland native says: "I started noticing some dramatic changes in my life. I was in medical sales at the time, and customers that I hadn't called on for months were calling me. Two large facilities that I had been calling on for more than five years closed almost effortlessly. I noted that my husband was becoming more verbally appreciative. The changes were noticeable enough that I began to research gratitude to see if there was something more to it. I discovered a lot of research that confirmed the truth behind what I was experiencing."

While studying appreciation and focusing on what she was grateful for, Lisa flashed back to an earlier time, when she was approaching her 30th birthday. She remembers how she had been going through a rough patch and was living in a funk. She gloomily observed that most of her friends were married, drove nice cars, and were starting to have families. She, on the other hand, was single, renting a house, leasing a car, and living with her four cats. It wasn't until it dawned on her that NOT having a husband, house, or car gave her freedom and flexibility that her friends did not have. Then she understood that these were actually the BEST times of her life. By being grateful for her life as it was, she experienced a complete *turnaround in her attitude. Because of the research she had begun, she understood why.*

With the power of gratitude as her driving force, Lisa says she finally had a purpose, a passion, and a sense that she could make a difference. Inspired by the personal coach guru Robbins, she was renewed to keep taking chances and pledged, "I want to have a career as a public speaker helping corporations understand the power of gratitude."

When she was downsized from what had once seemed an "incredibly successful" medical sales career, she made a decision to launch Grategy and share the information and research she had found about the transformational power of gratitude in the corporate world. To say her goal was pooh-poohed is to understate. "I remember one woman patting my arm and saying to me, 'You can't really expect to make money doing that can you?'"

"My mission is to change the face of business, one 'thank you' at a time," she says. She created a few key strategies (see sidebar) on cultivating gratitude in the workplace that she says will create a more engaged workplace, leading to higher employee satisfaction and an increased bottom line.

"As first, this topic of corporate gratitude and appreciation was seen as 'soft and fluffy.' However, in the years since I have been sharing this message, I have noticed a definite turnaround. The number of research projects and articles on employee engagement is growing exponentially, and businesses are starting to understand how important this issue is in the workplace."

At the same time, Lisa has experienced the transformation of gratitude in her personal life. One of the most memorable and heartfelt gifts of appreciation came from her ex-husband, Jeff, who called her when he was losing his battle with stage four cancer and knew he had a short time to live.

"He called to say goodbye," she says. "We had a brief conversation and said our final farewell." But then a statement that she used in many of her talks came back to haunt her. "Oftentimes, I tell my audiences that it should be illegal for people to say something during a eulogy that they did not say to that person while they were still on the planet." She asked herself, "Did I say everything to Jeff that I would have said at his eulogy?" and she realized that the answer was "No." Instead of saying, "Oh, well, I don't want to bother him again," she called him back. "We had a lovely talk about what we were most grateful for about each other in our lives," she says. "When we hung up the phone, everything we wanted to say was spoken. We were complete."

Months later, she was speaking at a corporation about embracing gratitude in the workplace, and she shared the story about her ex-husband. A man came up to her after the conference and told her how, throughout his wife's illness and during her final months, her pending death was the elephant in the room. "He said they weren't allowed to talk about it, so his wife died not knowing how grateful he was for her."

"It could so be easy to tell someone how grateful you are, yet we don't," she says. "The goal of my work is to spread the message about how important it is to help others feel validated and appreciated, especially in the place we spend our daily lives, our workplaces."

Fast-forward five years after initiating her research on gratitude. After leaving behind a sales career spanning more than 20 years, she transformed herself into the Chief Appreciation Strategist and Founder of Grategy. She is the author of six books including *The Upside of Down Times: Discovering the Power of Gratitude,* which was featured in the *New York Times* bestselling author Harvey Mackay's syndicated column "Swim With the Sharks Without Getting Eaten Alive." She co-starred in two films, including the award-winning *The Keeper of the Keys,* with Jack Canfield, of the *Chicken Soup for the Soul* series.

Lisa knows that she is still at the tip of the iceberg, but she feels that, by continuing to bring her message to the corporate world, she will truly change the face of business, one "thank you" at a time.

GRATEFUL LIFE PRACTICE

Today, think about the workers who support your organization in unseen ways. It may be the custodian who comes in at night to clean up. It may be the outside accounting firm who keeps the books and issues the paychecks. If you work at a nonprofit, it might be the families who donated money in honor of their deceased loved ones. You can express appreciation directly to these people in the form of a written note or a phone call. Even taking the time to thank them in your mind can help shift your thoughts from entitlement to gratitude—for the work that others do to make your job easier.

NINE-TO-FIVE:
WAYS TO CULTIVATE GRATITUDE AT WORK

Why should anyone thank you for just doing your job? And why should you ever thank your co-workers for doing what they're paid to do? These are common questions in American workplaces, often posed with hostility. Everywhere else in our lives we say thank you to honor the good things other people do for us. But not at work, according to a survey of 2,000 Americans by the John Templeton Foundation. They found that the workplace is where people are less likely than anywhere else—school, home, etc.—to express their gratitude.

It's not that people don't care, says Lisa Ryan. In fact almost 95 percent of those surveyed said that grateful bosses are more likely to succeed, and that they'd be more motivated to succeed if they were ever told they were appreciated.

Ryan suggests that the benefits of gratitude at work include a sense of self-worth, self-efficacy, and trust between employees. She gives tips for building a culture of gratitude at work in her "Take Your THANKS to the Bank" program, a six-step process to create a culture of appreciation in the workplace:

T = TRUST is the foundation of a productive work environment. Employees are watching their manager's actions more than they are listening to what their managers have to say. When there is congruence, there is trust. Expressing your sincere appreciation builds confidence and broadens trust in management.

H = HELP your staff identify their career path within the organization. Be proactive. Ask about their professional aspirations and work out a plan to help them attain their goals. When you ask employees what they want from the organization, you may discover skills, abilities, and interest that you didn't know existed.

A = APPLAUD the efforts of your team members. Be specific in your praise and in how their actions were beneficial to the firm. Put your appreciation in writing whenever possible.

N = NAVIGATE work / life balance. Look for ways to accommodate employees in getting their work done. When possible, explore options such as telecommuting, flexhours, and comp time. Managers should also be examples of work / life balance.

K = KNOW your staff. Listen to and show interest in your team members. Treat them the way they want to be treated. Respect their boundaries, and let them know that you are there when they need you.

S = SERVE your team. Create an environment of service that permeates all levels of the organization.

Ryan says: "When your employees trust you, they perform at a higher level. When you help them envision their career path, staff members engage. When you applaud their efforts, they are proud to work for you. When you help them navigate work / life balance issues, you reduce their stress. When you get to know them, you make them feel significant. And when you serve them, they feel included in the process. Harness the power of THANKS, and your organization will reap the rewards.

CREATING A CULTURE OF GRATITUDE:
HOW ONE WOMAN IS CULTIVATING
CONTENTMENT IN THE WORKPLACE

Gratitude is an inward expression of what your heart is yearning for.

—Ellen Miller

Ellen Miller was in the mood to make some changes in her life and get some inspiration.

The year was 2007, and the corporate speaker, trainer, and coach was attending an industry conference, when one of the participants proposed launching a new cause: "creating a complaint-free world."

Something didn't feel right about that statement for the Austin, Texas, entrepreneur, who says she's innately a "glass-half-full, positive thinker." She immediately reframed the thinking: "What if we launched a cause that was focused on finding the positive, what we're grateful for?"

remembers Ellen, founder of TEAM Performance, where she advises companies and partners to adopt employee engagement and positivity as the fabric of their culture.

At the same time, Ellen was extricating herself from a drama-filled and just-wrong relationship and trying to make the 10-hour trek from Austin, where she was living, to Kansas City, Missouri, to be present for her mother, who was losing her fight against lung cancer. "I was losing my mother, my rock," Ellen says.

Anticipatory grief is tough, but in taking care of her mom, Freda, it seemed that her whole hometown was showing up to express their gratitude for the difference Freda had made in their lives. Ellen realized what a mentor and role model her mom, a trailblazing real estate business woman in the early 1960s, had been in her life and to so many others.

She realized she could focus on the loss, or she could do as her mom had always inspired her: Go get 'em, go make her dreams come true. After her mom passed, she realized what she needed to do: Spread the blessings and lessons she'd learned, about celebrating gratefulness, to others. The Grateful Heart Movement was born.

Expressions of gratitude in the workplace aren't exactly a common practice, says Ellen. That's why she reinvented her coaching and business training practice into a movement to teach companies how to build a thankful organization.

"About six months after my mom's passing, I was still so sorrowful, but I realized I had to turn this around and do something with that energy to celebrate the values she instilled in me," she says. "She always told me to go for my dreams and was such a role model as a business woman for me. I realized I was trying to create motivational strategies for businesses, and that a new goal for me would be to spread the message of the practice of being grateful in the workplace."

She launched the Grateful Heart Movement, creating workshops and a methodology for businesses to drive their success through the lens of gratefulness, appreciation, and possibility. Part of the project targeted teaching gratitude to daycare providers—and to the kids in their care. It's an experiment Ellen hopes to introduce to people in all kinds of careers, and to instill the idea of appreciating what you have in life in children at an early age. She also created a product line to help others more easily be reminded of their grateful-driven mission: gratitude bracelets, journals, and more.

She says, "To live in gratefulness first takes an understanding of your own current thinking. Do you look at things with scarcity (there's not enough for everyone, so I need to make sure I get my share) in mind? Or do you approach things believing there is a win-win possible in every situation? Understanding where you are now can help you create a mind-set of gratitude. Then look at others, such as Mother Teresa, Oprah Winfrey, school-teachers, and community volunteers, who have served as great role models for the next step in creating a grateful heart mind-set. Take the action to give of yourself to others."

Ellen also created a business strategy for making gratitude stick and transform thinking. Her guiding principles include:

Live. Commit to live inside your grateful heart. Promote goodwill, inner peace, joy, and gratitude in yourself, and look for ways to share them and benefit others.

Act. A grateful mind-set starts with you. Act with a grateful heart and share your gratitude with others to multiply the impact. Approach every interaction with the intention to promote an attitude of gratitude.

Express. Journal what you are grateful for each day for two minutes. Share with at least one person daily what you appreciate about them. Do a random act of kindness each day for someone in need.

Live...Act...Express. Do the above three things for 90 days and see how your life transforms. When life happens, reach for gratefulness, as it is nearly impossible to be in negativity when you are truly grateful. We hope you all will open your hearts and join this amazing journey in gratefulness.

One caveat, she says: "Gratefulness is not a one-time thing that you do and then you're done. It's an ongoing process that opens up new worlds of opportunity in work, love, friendships, service, and humanity."

Good news: Ellen practices what she preaches. Months after her mom died, the 50-something biz exec says she "called on her mom" to help her find a companion to share her life. Today, she lives with the "love of my life," Jack.

"I incorporated gratitude into my everyday life and have watched the positive effects ripple throughout all areas of my life," she says. "Over time, I moved back home to be with my family. I entered into a new relationship. I expanded my business. I improved my health and fitness. My life, my relationships, my friendships—my whole existence has become better than I could have ever imagined."

GRATEFUL LIFE PRACTICE
One of Ellen's missions is to work with daycare providers to help them impart the lessons of gratitude to preschool children. What are some of the things you can do to teach young children how to give thanks for what they have, instead of taking everything they have for granted? Children learn from example, and one of the best ways is to model your own grateful behavior. Thank them for their actions—for instance, for picking up their toys or cooperating with others on the playground. Share with them your gratitude for the small things in life. You can do with your own children, or even with strangers. The more gratitude children are exposed to, the more it will become a part of their reality.

FRIENDS RALLY TOWNS TO TRANSFORM STREET ART INTO THE GRATITUDE GRAFFITI PROJECT

Living your life through gratitude is not one of comparing how you are better than someone else; or gratitude only for what you own or obtain or achieve. Living your life through gratitude is seeing that the world would be missing something very unique and valuable if you were not in it.

—Sumner M. Davenport

The handwritten messages penned in a rainbow of colors with washable markers were spreading fast across the storefronts, libraries, and community buildings all around Maplewood, Highland Park, Teaneck, and several other New Jersey cities.

"I am grateful for the happy things in life," reads one note.

"I am grateful to live in a peace-loving community," reads a note left in the window of a comics store.

"I am glad my son is safely back at home."

"I am glad it is a good day and the sun is shining."

"I am grateful for my accident—it gave me the pause to slow down and observe my life."

"I am grateful for my little brother Joey," one child wrote while visiting her brother at the hospital.

The missives were touching and profound. They are part of the Gratitude Graffiti project—part community-wide art project, part exercise in appreciating the everyday.

The Gratitude Graffiti Project was started in the fall of 2012 by Candice Davenport and Lucila McElroy, close friends who met when their collective six (three each) grade-school-age kids were in classes together. It is based on a simple concept, supported by positive psychology research and literature, that one of the most important steps to wellness and happiness is to assume a daily practice of gratitude.

Their goal was to create a reminder by utilizing community hubs ("Gratitude Stops") to creatively engage each passerby and member of the community to take a moment to be grateful for a minimum of 40 days.

It was meant to be a small, community-wide gesture. More than 23 stores and libraries participated the first year. But by year two the project had flourished into a larger organic movement in the practice of mindfulness and gratitude in more than 100 locations, including storefronts, libraries, schools, food banks, coffee shops, hospice centers, rehab facilities, community *organizations, and hospitals. The project is now found throughout New Jersey, Pennsylvania, New York, California, and internationally in Vancouver, British Columbia, and Hong Kong, with almost 300 community members across the globe on Facebook.*

Candice, a nurse and public health educator, and Lucila, a life coach, were moms who met on the playground of their children's school in Maplewood, New Jersey. But at the same time they were experiencing life-changing transformation under the surface of their own lives. They both realized how they were experiencing firsthand in their own personal and professional lives that practicing a daily habit of being grateful for what they had was creating a sense of happiness and well-being.

In her healthcare / public health practice, Candice had grown to believe that a sense of place and the messages that surround us can affect the human condition. Various fields of science support that we're all connected to each other and how our actions can have a positive impact on each other. Because she is a health educator and a creative writer, she has experienced firsthand how physically engaging in an art process can create a mind-body-spirit connection as well as an uplifting experience.

The year before, when Lucila made a trip to New York City, she noticed some cool murals that caught her attention. One included a string with chalk and asked passersby to write: "Before I die_____." Another was a parking sign where people had written what they were hopeful for. "They made a strong impact on me as I walked by," remembers Lucila.

Lucila had also had the experience of looking for the perfect gift for her husband's 40th birthday. She and her three daughters, ages eight, 10, and 12, came up with the idea of "Forty Days to Express His Greatness." Every day, for 40 days leading up to her husband, Kevin's, birthday, they gave him cards, notes, links to his favorite songs, cycling lessons, and other things he could open on his business travels. For his birthday, the family went on a cycling trip. Though the gift was a big hit with her husband, it shifted something inside of Lucila, who last year moved from Maplewood to Vancouver.

"I noticed a change in *me*," she says. "People always say I'm a glass-half-full person, but there was a new peacefulness. I experienced a definite shift, and I couldn't pinpoint why."

It took one turning-point conversation on their first meeting to realize that, while Lucila wanted to spread the good news about the power of gratitude, Candice saw art as the perfect way to engage their community and have people participate in it in a very accessible and fun way.

"As moms we saw how our children learn by playing and expressing themselves, how they hit their stride in a run, and that movement can be a spark of genius," says

Candice. "As adults, we both realized that playing around the fringes of art, plus a practice of mindfulness, can be a way for us to 're-create,' to rejuvenate ourselves, and that it can lead to a better state of health and wellness."

They decided to make it a community-wide effort and set off on foot to convince the shop owners, teachers, librarians, and community leaders that their shop windows could become a canvas of gratitude with artistically written expressions of gratitude: a virtual living work of art created by the community that would easily wipe away after the 40 days leading up to Thanksgiving.

"We figured this was affordable—all you needed was a storefront window to create the canvas," says Lucila. "It was also a project that could be all-inclusive. The elderly, children, anyone could participate, and it would affirm how we are all connected by our humanity and yet unique in our individuality, as seen in the varying thoughts of gratitude."

It didn't take much convincing, and the Gratitude Graffiti Project was born.

"When we asked store owners no one resisted," the duo chimes in together. "They realize that when people come into a place with these messages on their windows, it creates a good feeling, they're in a good place."

The idea was simple but significant. Through the Gratitude Graffiti Project, participants are no longer "spectators" of art, they are fully engaged in creating the art that expresses their gratitude. "Through art, people can contemplate, create, rejuvenate, and awaken a whole new perspective on how to look at how great life can be," says Lucila.

For 40 days, stores that participated, dubbed "Gratitude Stops," marked their windows so that passersby could post their expressions of gratitude. People walking by can read what others are grateful for, mentally note something they are grateful for, or to take it a step further by actively writing or drawing what they are grateful for that day on a on a storefront window or on a "Gratitude Graffiti" wall with a Post-it note. The Gratitude Stops become living works of art, reflective of individual and community gratefulness, for all to see.

"It's like an old-fashioned Tweet," says Candice. "When you put it out there, it makes you stop and reflect on what you are grateful for, but when you are sitting in a hospital lobby or walk into a store and see these, something magical happens to you." Lucila adds, "It taps deeply into the hearts and minds of people."

There's also something transformational about being inside a shop and observing someone pen their message, the friends agree. "When you are observing someone from the other side of the window, they are in their own thought; they do not even see you. As an observer you can't help but feel joy for the other person when they take a step back and realize: 'I just wrote that.' You see an immediate reaction: their shoulders relax; they laugh or smile. And you watch them just take it all in, the significance of what they've just done."

Different places also found different and creative ways to manifest the project. The library version called, "Due Date for Gratitude," lets people post sticky Post-it notes up and down the windows and walls of the main lobby. It was covered from floor to ceiling. Others used sidewalk chalk, or ribbons hanging from their window or along the school fence.

Lucila and Candice posted a listing of charities organizations could use to jump-start the project. "Thank you for visiting the Gratitude Graffiti Project website," they wrote. "If you are practicing daily gratitude but want to jump-start your practice, our recommendation is to try donating your time, energy, and talents to one of the following local (and not so local) charities."

In the end, Candice and Lucila believe that the project gives people the opportunity to see the world differently. "Even when times are tough, it gives you the opportunity to see what you do have in your life. Your house floods, but you are grateful that you can call a plumber and it can be fixed. Or friends show up to support you," says Lucila.

"The project has shown that a community-wide practice of gratitude can create a healthier community. It can also be an important part of a healing and growth process. It seems like such a simple gesture, but sharing a single thought of thankfulness can mean the world to someone you may never meet, and that's one of the beautiful things about the project," adds Candice.

Lucila now teaches in schools in Vancouver about looking at life through a lens of gratitude and how that can change your perspective on life. The words of a fellow school mom about the project speak volumes to its success. The mom reported that she had been having a very tough day and was pretty angry in the car driving home. Her daughter, who had participated in the gratitude project, said to her, "Mom, what glasses are you wearing today?" Her daughter's words were a wake-up call to this mom to speak and experience life through the lens of gratitude. "The mom told us she was practically crying when her daughter said that," says Lucila. "She thanked us and said, 'I took off my angry glasses.'"

What's next for these gratitude-preneurs? They've named 2014 the year of gratitude and plan to meet somewhere between Vancouver and New Jersey, perhaps Chicago, next fall to spread the good news about gratitude with hopes that it will grow and become a national tradition around the Thanksgiving holiday.

GRATEFUL LIFE PRACTICE

Want to spread an attitude of gratitude into the world you live? Launch a Gratitude Graffiti Project in your town in your schools, libraries, or hospitals. All it takes is erasable markers and a willingness to reach out to community leaders to ask them to come on board. To learn more about how you can launch a Gratitude Graffiti Project in your hometown visit their website: thegratitudegraffitiproject.com

CHAPTER FOUR

HOW ALTRUISM EVOKES GRATITUDE, WHICH SPREADS HAPPINESS

We make a living by what we get. We make a life by what we give.

—Winston Churchill

Karma is an ancient Indian concept that links a person's actions to their destiny. This belief, that "what goes around, comes around," is especially true when it comes to giving. It's been said that grateful people are more giving, perhaps because they want to share the abundance they appreciate in their own lives.

Grateful living, which is conducive to generosity whether in the form of gifts or volunteering, has been scientifically proven to increase joy. So is it truly altruism, if there are so many ways that giving promotes personal growth? We don't care about semantics—we only know that practicing charity and benevolence makes the world a better place and is a surefire way to reduce anxiety and increase joy.

Science supports this too. A 2008 study by Harvard Business School professor Michael Norton and colleagues found that giving money to someone else lifted participants' happiness more than spending it on themselves. Giving back also releases positive endorphins in the brain. Volunteering and doing charity work—as we saw in the story about Cristina Peczon who feeds abandoned and orphaned children each year on her birthday—also set a great example for the young people in one's life.

Giving has a ripple effect that can spread by three degrees. A study by James Fowler at the University of California, San Diego, and Nicholas Christakis of Harvard, shows that when one person behaves generously, it inspires observers to behave generously later, toward different people. "As a result," they write, "each person in a network can influence dozens or even hundreds of people, some of whom he or she does not know and has not met."

This holds true even in countries where sharing with others might threaten someone's own subsistence! In one study, the researchers examined data about more than 200,000 people from 136 countries; they determined that donating to charity boosts happiness across all cultures and levels of economic well-being. It was even true regardless of whether someone said they'd had trouble securing food for their family in the past year.

When the researchers zeroed in on three countries with vastly different levels of wealth—Canada, Uganda, and India—they found that people reported greater happiness when they'd spent money on others than when they'd spent on themselves. In fact, they argue, the nearly universal emotional benefits of altruism suggest it is a product of evolution, perpetuating behavior that "may have carried short-term costs but long-term benefits for survival over human evolutionary history." So the more you give, the more you open within yourself the space to receive.

You may find that giving feels better than receiving. As Dr. Wayne W. Dyer wrote in a post on HealYourLife.com, "Perhaps the surest way to find happiness and joy for yourself is to devote your energies toward making someone else happy. If you make an effort to search for joy you will find it elusive, largely because you will become engaged in the search itself. Your life will be about striving. However, if you try to bring happiness to someone else, then joy will come to you."

LIVING LIFE IN THE GRATEFUL LANE:
THE ROAD GETS ROUGH, BUT THIS RUNNER NEVER FALTERS

*The greatest glory in living, lies not in never fall-
ing, but in rising every time we fall.*

—South African President Nelson Mandela

*For 50 years Tom Zimmerman, 70, has been passionate
about the sport of running. Before running was in vogue,
this Chicago resident sprinted along the shores of Lake
Michigan in searing heat, snow, and ice. He has participated in countless competitions and continues to compete
in 5K charity runs, including a New Year's Day 5K, a
fund-raiser for the Lincoln Park Zoo in Chicago, and
the Lincolnwood Turkey Trot, which supports a scholarship fund for struggling families. Beloved by many for his
optimism, authenticity, and sense of humor, Tom made a
conscious decision—at the same time he began running—*

to view the proverbial glass as always "half full." He describes his past as a series of fortuitous events that add up to a charmed life. Tom likens himself to a successful gambler, blessed with good fortune throughout his life. Until the day he couldn't run.

Tom remembers being "stunned" after receiving a diagnosis of acute myeloid leukemia (AML) in September 2010 after a lifetime of excellent health. But true to his character, his next thought was, "Let's move on. I'm not going to feel sorry for myself." He wasn't fearful about the illness or the induction therapy. It was the break from his routine—not being able to run—that finally got him down. His room at Northwestern Memorial Hospital looked out on the running path along Lake Michigan, and one day he asked his doctor, "Do you think I will ever do that again?" His young doctor replied, "Yes. Yes, you will." That message of hope enabled him to prevail through the rest of his treatment, a bout with pneumonia, and a very difficult decision to refuse a stem cell transplant.

Today Tom can be found back on track, running his beloved paths, and volunteering for the Leukemia & Lymphoma Society's Team in Training and Leukemia Cup Regatta, the Chicago Marathon, Lincoln Park Zoo, and numerous other local organizations. Here he shares his secrets for moving on, even when the going gets rough.

Chance meetings—such as one with a future employer after Tom's graduation from Mundelein College of Loyola University in 1970—have been a staple of Tom Zimmerman's life. While on vacation in Monterrey, Mexico, Tom was on his way to the next city when a hurricane grounded everyone at the airport. He stopped in a bar, where he engaged in a conversation with Mr. Sanchez, who ran a school focused on teaching English to business leaders anxious to expand to the U.S. marketplace. Mr. Sanchez asked Tom if he might be interested. He took the opportunity. This was just the first of what he terms lucky breaks that are entwined with Tom's commitment to optimism and gratitude.

"I wasn't born upbeat and positive," he says. "I made a conscious decision early on in my adult life that nothing was ever going to get me down." He says that he "really believes that good things will happen to me," and "whatever I've needed in terms of jobs, people, strengths, they've always come through." Tom's practice of attracting abundance is rooted in gratitude for everything he's been given.

He has had his share of travails. Tom was the oldest of six. His youngest sister experienced sudden-onset schizophrenia in 1982. "One day, my sister was a normal, happy, pleasant person," he says. "The next minute, she couldn't talk, and was put in restraints." Tom also went through a divorce, and recently fought a tough battle with cancer. To meet Tom, though, is to meet someone who is always laughing, always happy, and always grateful.

His lifelong career in book publishing stemmed from what he terms a "lucky break" when a sales position opened up with the company he was writing for—William C. Brown Company Publishers—where he remained for the next 15 years. Another fortuitous event occurred when Tom was newly single at age 50 and decided that his soul mate was "out there somewhere," so he developed a strategy to find her. According to Tom, he budgeted $5,000 for this "project," and dated a number of women. Just when he was down to the last $100 of his budget, he called a woman named Sherry who had placed an ad in *The Reader,* an alternative weekly paper in Chicago. As he looked at the personals, one ad stood out above the rest. It described qualities sought in a partner such as "gracious, spiritual, compassionate…, and employed." He left a humorous message requesting a call. He described himself as having "a full head of hair, a job, and all of his teeth."

This was in January. In April he picked up the phone, and the person on the line sweetly said, "This is Sherry—do you remember me?" They both began to laugh. Sherry said she had been filing some old papers and came across his message and thought he was funnier on the phone than most people she had been on dates with. They married 18 months later, and today, over 18 years later, they remain soul mates.

Together, Tom and Sherry faced the most difficult choice in Tom's life when he had to decide whether to have a stem cell transplant after his chemotherapy consolidation treatments. "It wasn't like choosing the lesser of two evils—both options were equally evil," he says. "I talked to everyone I could, hoping that someone would say something to tip the scales." Nothing helped, until he decided to let his love of running settle the score. "What finally helped me decide to skip the stem cell transplant was my desire to have just one ordinary week, one ordinary month," he says. "My oncologist told me that I'd have to be in it 100 percent in order for it to be successful. After eight months of treatments and complications, my heart was not in it." Fortunately, his sister Margaret is an exact match should he need a stem cell transplant. "I call her my 'lease to joy,' " he says. "She has given me the freedom to get well."

Today, over three years since his diagnosis, Tom is in fine health. Always a grateful person, he says this experience has moved him to greater depths of appreciation for the small things.

"I remember after the induction therapy, I came out of the hospital, and noticed the leaves falling off the trees, shrubs preparing for the winter, flowers long past their summer beauty," he describes. "I started crying, because it was all so beautiful, just breathing the air felt so good." Another experience that moved him deeply occurred after his cousin's girlfriend Nicole, who works at the hospital, stopped by to see Tom before he was discharged. He was overcome with gratitude and poignantly pronounced, "So many people have done so much for me. How do I ever repay it?" Nicole simply responded, "You will find a way."

From that day forward, Tom has filled his days with "giving back." But he doesn't consider it charity. Instead, he feels like he is living his dream by volunteering at the Lincoln Park Zoo on projects like the West Nile Virus Surveillance System and the Serengeti Health Initiative in the Conservation and Science group. "I feel so privileged to work with epidemiologists and animal research specialists who are dedicated to helping endangered species," he says. "I've always had an interest in science, and I am so grateful to be able to play even a very small part in making the world a better place for future generations."

He also volunteers for the Team in Training program for the Leukemia & Lymphoma Society, the world's largest voluntary health agency dedicated to blood cancer, by participating in fund-raising events and cheering on runners at the Chicago Marathon. He and his wife, Sherry, are "Chicago Greeters," part of Choose Chicago, the city organization responsible for marketing the greater Chicago area as a business and leisure visitor destination. Visitors to Chicago can sign up for a personal tour of the downtown area or a particular neighborhood. "The best part of this is to see the city I love through 'outside' eyes," he says. "Recently a woman from San Francisco rendezvoused with her son—a resident of New York—in Chicago. They were both seasoned travelers, and were so enthusiastic about every aspect of their tour. At the end of the tour, the woman turned to me and said that she loved the city so much she wanted to retire here!"

Tom is also a ham radio operator, and during his runs he says he first practices Morse code, and "then I mentally review all the tours Sherry and I give as part of the Chicago Greeters program. This is the only way I can remember the details of tour routes, the locations of public art, architectural history, and historical sites. A three-hour walking tour in my head takes almost five miles of running. It's rehearsal time."

When asked for advice about how others can learn from his example, Tom characteristically notes that he is always learning from others. "I learned so much from volunteering at the zoo, particularly from one woman who was a Conservation and Science Coordinator." He joined in on one of her behavioral studies and observed how she meticulously took time to track the movements of the Sichuan takins, a goat antelope found in China. "She would carefully observe where they were, what they were doing, and how they moved about," he continues. "That taught me a very important lesson. She showed me that, if you want to appreciate something, you have to take the time to really look and really listen. That secret, if you will, enriches your appreciation of everything."

Tom considers himself a very lucky person. Have you ever asked yourself how some people "get to be lucky"?

We've excerpted this piece with permission from the author Bob Miglani because we think it answers that very question. Bob Miglani is the author of a book titled *Embrace the Chaos*, and you can find his blog at www.embracethechaos.com.

21 REASONS WHY SOME PEOPLE GET SO LUCKY IN LIFE

Did you ever look at someone and think, "He is so lucky. He has money, he's in a great relationship, and wow—what a great career being able to travel like that"?

I've done it too. And, as my mind entertained this thought, I would find myself in an often depressing place over thinking about reasons why I wasn't as successful as "that guy."

I wasn't so lucky. I wasn't lucky to be born with good looks or into the right family. I wasn't lucky enough to have the right education or to be at the right place at the right time.

But as I grew in my career and in my life, and by meeting lots of people from all over the world in so many walks of life, I came to this profound realization:

Sure, we can be born into it and fall into it. But so many successful people I've met—from couples in blissful long-term relationships to successful career women to billionaires to profoundly happy people who have very little—became "lucky" because they think differently and take certain actions.

As I thought about my own journey of learning to deal with uncertainty these days, I realized that in the absence of luck being granted to us by the lottery of birth, we all can get a chance to get lucky. Here are 21 reasons why some people get lucky in life.

Lucky people...

1. Work hard...quietly. They don't boast, toast, or celebrate. They do. Toiling away at their craft day in and day out. They don't announce it on Facebook or tweet about it on Twitter. Lucky people get busy working.

2. Surround themselves with positive people who build them up not tear them down. Life is hard enough as it is, without having to worry about negative people slowing you down.

3. Put positive seeds into their mind every single day. All of us wake up with sometimes random thoughts that can debilitate. By proactively choosing the right words and actions, some people overcome those morning limitations set by the mind. They have certain rituals. A morning run, meditation, prayer, or their morning cup of coffee while walking the dog.

4. Fight the over-thinking mind each day. You are not alone. We all over-think choices that lie ahead. It can

be a daily battle. Is it in our DNA? Maybe. But increasingly I've learned that some people—especially happier people—make a choice to limit their over-thinking mind.

5. Have a clear purpose. Lucky people have a crystal-clear objective. Either to provide more for their children than they had growing up, or to successfully launch their business. Whatever their cause, lucky people have a magnet attracting them to their goals.

6. Accept imperfection. They don't say, "It's not a good time right now." But they do say, "It's always a good time right here and right now." They know the right time will never come to them. They have to go out and make it the right time.

7. Don't gossip or pay attention to the critics. Lucky people don't get distracted by the naysayers, doubters, or haters. They don't allow the negativity to enter their mind. Shrugging off a desire to gossip or respond to critics, lucky people smile and keep walking forward.

8. Feel more than they think. They are often driven by emotion and passion about their endeavor. Thinking is important, but often we let our minds direct us forward. And when we face a difficult circumstance, we are conflicted between what we think and what we feel. Lucky people seem to lead from the heart, not the head.

9. Focus on the goal, not the plan. Plans can change. Chaos can interrupt the best laid plans. But goals don't. Happy marriage, talented kids, meaningful work, and a

successful career—these usually remain constant. But how we get there can change over time.

10. Take lots of action. Lucky people have a bias for trying things, even if they may fail. They create certainty by moving forward rather than sitting still. Momentum goes when your energy flows.

11. Are open to meeting anyone, anytime. Talking openly to anyone who'll listen to their ideas, lucky people smile and engage—opening up their minds to chance meetings with strangers where one thing can lead to another.

12. Remain in the day-to-day. Letting go of the past and focusing on the present moments, lucky people direct their effort at what they can control right here and right now, not worrying as much about yesterday or tomorrow.

13. Get hurt by the setbacks and the failures as much as anyone, but they keep going because they know that they'll come out of it. They have this powerful belief that tough times pass and that, if they persevere long enough, they'll get through the failures.

14. Believe in themselves. They're not arrogant. Lucky people feel that all of us have this inner strength, this resiliency of the human mind that can achieve great things.

15. Are always curious, asking questions about the simplest things to everyone they know. They want to understand how things work. They are explorers wanting to get to the bottom of things. They welcome new ideas, thoughts or observations.

16. Know that getting to success is never a straight line but a path full of curves and side roads. Lucky people zigzag their way through life, often in uncharted waters.

17. Are grateful. Recognizing that life is not a right but a gift, lucky people act with great humility.

18. Admit that they're not that smart. Lucky people become smart and learn by trying. They read. They toil. Admit their faults. Apologize quickly and move on. They recognize that happiness and success in life come from constant learning.

19. Serve others. Many things, from launching a new business to sustaining a happy marriage, require serving someone besides yourself. Lucky people give generously to others through their effort in their jobs, their careers, their business and personal lives. Their effort is focused on ensuring others have what they need before their own needs are met.

20. Know that they're not born lucky. They become lucky by studying, working, and refining their craft. Lucky people don't count on luck. They make the choice to think differently and to take action.

21. Are hungry. They want it badly. They believe they have something of value to give to the world and are aching to give it. Lucky people jump out of bed in the morning. They sacrifice—giving up the luxuries of the modern world (TV, Facebook, etc.)—so that they can get to work fulfilling the promise they make to themselves.

BREAKING POINTE: YOU CAN'T STOP THIS DANCER. GRATITUDE BECOMES BEST PRACTICE FOR RECOVERY AND RESOLVE TO HELP OTHERS

Twenty-one-year-old Cynthia Toussaint was warming up at the barre during ballet class at the University of California, Irvine, when it happened. She elongated her body, reaching up to stretch her back. Pop! Like a guitar string being plucked, something snapped in the back of her right leg. Despite the occasional bout of tendinitis or a pulled muscle, she hadn't suffered a serious injury and didn't have a lot of patience with other dancers she deemed less than stoic. "Ballerinas are told to smile and get through," she remembers thinking.

But that day in 1982 changed her world, shattering

her aspirations to become a ballerina, singer, and actress and thrusting her into the world of chronic pain. It is a silent and invisible disease that haunts both those who suffer from the pain and the caregivers who strive to stay at their sides.

Cynthia and her boyfriend, John Garrett, found themselves housebound in their 20s as John took over full-time caregiving. "You start losing contact with people and the natural progression of life," says John. He admits his fantasy was to hop in his Honda Civic and flee. "It was so overwhelming on so many levels," he says. "Watching a person suffer is psychologically difficult; it drags the caregiver with them and leaves no survivors, and it sucks everything in."

After 13 years and myriad X-rays, doctor's visits, and one hospital stay, Cynthia was diagnosed with complex regional pain syndrome (CRPS), a chronic pain condition most often affecting arms, legs, hands, or feet, usually after an injury or trauma to that limb. She would learn that the hamstring injury had triggered the disease.

But the North Hollywood, California, couple pushed through and turned the despair and hopeless into the pursuit of new dreams.

Today, Cynthia says she feels lucky because she is one of the few persons she knows whose partner-turned-caregiver stayed with her during the decades she has been in pain. In the 20 years since her diagnosis, (nearly 32 years since the accident), she has gradually learned to live a full life despite her chronic illness and pain.

Determined to lean on grace and gratitude to push through, Cynthia founded For Grace (www.forgrace. org), an organization dedicated to empowering women to be better consumers for their pain management care. As an activist, she's spearheaded and given key testimony at two California Senate hearings—one dedicated to CRPS awareness, the second exploring the chronic under-treatment of and gender bias toward women in pain—and has hosted an annual Women in Pain Conference in Los Angeles since 2008. The event brings together hundreds of women in pain, their caregivers, and the healthcare professionals who treat them, as well as experts in pain management, psychology, and advocacy to explore and investigate chronic pain and the spectrum of coping choices one has to make to endure and thrive with this daunting health challenge. Cynthia also believes it is vital to share what she's learned along the way and has chronicled her journey from pain to advocate in her book, Battle for Grace: A Memoir of Pain, Redemption and Impossible Love (Forgrace.org, 2013)

"My life was perfect then," Cynthia recalls about her days in college when she was pursuing her dream as a ballerina and actress and had just met the guy she knew would be the love of her life.

But then the accident thrust her into the world of 100 million—one-third of all Americans—who suffer from chronic pain. The pain lingered, and it became excruciating.

"Days, weeks, and years disappeared into the fire of my pain," she recalls. The ballerina could no longer pirouette, jeté, or even walk. Eventually, the hamstring injury healed. But the pain never went away, and it spread to her arms and vocal chords. It left her bedridden for a decade and unable to speak for five of those years.

"It made me feel as if I'd been doused with gasoline and lit on fire," she says. She feared she would never get better, would never walk again, and worst of all that she would never dance again. "Pain and fear became the essence of my existence."

As the years and months ticked by, the pain intensified. "People began avoiding me," she says. "As I watched people leave, I slipped into a depression that would last on and off for decades."

To get through it all, Cynthia tapped into her innate positivity, lifetime resilience, and ability to surface and find the blessings in the muck.

"I lost my father to suicide when I was eight, and being the middle child of five, I naturally took care of everyone," she says. "I held everything together. I learned great appreciation for what I had early on, so it comes naturally to me. When I got ill, I became aware of how many things can go wrong with our bodies and minds."

She made a conscious decision to focus instead on the positive.

"I have my eyesight and my hearing, my brain functions, my heart beats, on and on," she enthuses.

Her pain pushed her to realize she couldn't be the only one going through this kind of situation. One day, she asked herself, "What is happening to all the people like me who are living with CRPS long term?" As she started connecting to and hearing stories of others just like her, her life took another turn: She moved from victim to activist, deciding to form an organization to empower others like her.

"I pushed on despite the pain, even when it peaked," she says. "I'd lie in a reclining wheelchair to work at the computer and talk on the phone, scribbling notes as I crafted ideas. I was always amazed at how this work helped me 'forget' the pain," she continues. "During my occasional breaks, awareness of the pain filled the vacuum and I'd lie in my chair moaning. But, despite the pain and frenetic pace, I was happier than I'd been in years. I had purpose, a reason to get up."

Fast-forward almost 20 years, to today. Toussaint is currently experiencing her second partial CRPS remission and living with her life partner, John Garrett, in Los Angeles.

"It's a place that for almost 30 years I never thought possible," she says. And the best part is that she has regained some—not all—of her mobility. Though she can't dance, she can swim, sing, and perform a ballet-Pilates floor workout. "I can walk short distances, but have to use a wheelchair for anything more than about half a block," she adds.

But her remission doesn't mean she's pain free, and it doesn't mean she's forgotten her mission: "to help women in pain live, grow, and receive equal treatment from medical professionals."

For Cynthia, giving up is not an option. Until the accident, success was something that came naturally, that she achieved by performing.

"Success-wise, I've always been extremely determined, confident, and focused," she says. Her mom's influence and the discipline of ballet instilled in her a strong self-esteem that helped her believe she could achieve anything she set her mind to. "Not succeeding is not an option."

She also believes that what is done does with success matters, and quitting is not an option either. "When I thought I'd become a successful performer, I always planned on leveraging that into a cause that would help people," she says. Now she is accomplishing that with a twist—running a foundation for others who are also suffering from pain. Through her nonprofit organization, For Grace, she's created the support, community and awareness for women in chronic pain that she needed during the years she fought for doctors to take her condition seriously and pinpoint a diagnosis.

"I can't bear the suffering of others—and I can't imagine worse torture than what John and I have been through," she says. "I do everything in my power to save others from that fate. I've refocused my passion into the work I've created at For Grace. I never again want a woman in pain to feel alone and hopeless."

Now that she is doing better physically, she's putting her energy and passion back into performance of a different kind and with a different emphasis—to help her cause.

"I love being a leader and all that comes with it," she adds. "Being the decision-maker, sparking ideas, taking action, risk-taking, always staring fear down. I love it when people tell me I can't do something. 'Impossible,' they say. And that makes the success even sweeter."

At her side throughout this 31-year journey has been John, the love of her life and her greatest gift.

"When it comes to John, I've always believed that I deserve to be with this extraordinary man. I deserve a loving partner, as does he. As does everyone. John and I have DEEP love and respect for each other. Though we can't marry legally without losing my healthcare, we've made promises to each other—our 'vows'—and those vows are absolutely sacred. It's nothing either of us questions. John is my partner in everything. There cannot be a greater love. I'm so very blessed.

"Since I've pushed through to the other side, I've become much deeper, wiser, empathic, and peaceful. I care more about people, animals, and our planet. I'm grateful to still have the ability to do things I'm passionate about. My values have shifted. My heroes have evolved. It's less about me and more about everything else. I've learned that the only truly important thing in life is kindness."

GRATITUDE PRACTICE

To keep herself focused on the blessings in her life, Cynthia practices mindfulness meditation every day. And she prays. "It feels good to send out positive energies to others," she says. When Cynthia prays, she thanks the universe for "what I have been given." She adds, "That meditation and prayer is a daily reaffirmation, a reminder of what I'm blessed with—and that practice helps to keep me positive, centered, and forward-moving."

BEING ALRIGHT: DAUGHTER-TURNED-DOCTOR REACHES BACK TO HELP DOMESTIC VIOLENCE VICTIMS

Life without thankfulness is devoid of love and passion. Hope without thankfulness is lacking in fine perception. Faith without thankfulness lacks strength and fortitude. Every virtue divorced from thankfulness is maimed and limps along the spiritual road.

—John Henry Jowett

Sonia Oyola, M.D., is a mom of three children, ages nine to 13, and back-to-school season for her is always in full swing. Each year her personal to-do list gets longer and longer.

She takes pride when her trio is ready and raring to go for the new school year ahead. But that is also true for dozens of other Chicago-area youngsters who, thanks to the generosity of supporters Sonia has rallied, arrive in their classrooms each fall armed with brightly colored, brand-new backpacks and school supplies.

In the fall of 2013, 79 children living at Greenhouse

Shelter and several other domestic violence shelters throughout Chicago were the recipients of this back-to-school initiative, releasing moms living in shelters from the stressful financial burden of buying school supplies.

In 2009, Sonia founded Be Alright to support survivors of domestic violence at shelters throughout the Chicago area. The generosity of her troupe of angels extends far beyond fall to gifts for the shelter families during the winter holiday season, and on Mother's Day and throughout the year for moms at Connections for Abused Women and Their Children's Greenhouse Shelter and others.

For Sonia, assistant professor at the University of Illinois, Chicago, department of family medicine, domestic violence is a personal and passionate cause. The school backpacks and supplies speak volumes about the despair she felt as a young girl, arriving at school on Chicago's West Side, too poor to be equipped with the supplies other kids had and pained by the abuse going on in her family behind closed doors.

"It's so hard for these kids when there is so much chaos at home," she says. "I remember my first day of school, sitting in the back of the classroom hoping no one would notice me because I didn't have school supplies. We're just trying to bring a little sparkle, a sense of community and belonging."

* * *

In her medical practice, and through teaching health professionals and providing a little Christmas every day to kids and their moms through Be Alright, Sonia is a tireless advocate against domestic violence. She shares her story with women seeking help through Connections for Abused Women and their Children (CAWC) in the hope that it will help grow awareness and give voice to the one in four women who are victims of domestic violence and the 3 million children who witness this violence in their homes each year. CAWC runs Greenhouse Shelter, the largest domestic violence shelter in Chicago, with 42 beds and three cribs, all filled to capacity every night.

But unlike other victims and survivors, Sonia feels grateful that, in the midst of the family chaos, she was able to find her voice, to understand that domestic violence isn't okay, and to set her sights on dreams she would pursue in the future.

"I once was a little girl who witnessed what alcohol and abuse can do to a family," she says. "I learned that violence is not right. My mom let me have a voice and let me know it was not my fault. She gave permission to ask, 'Why is this happening?' "

At age two, she came to the United States from Colombia with her mother to reunite with her father, who had arrived a year earlier to work in a welding factory. Unfortunately, during the time away from his family, her father's isolation and loneliness drove him to drink, and he developed a problem with alcoholism. "When we arrived, my dad was a different person than the man my mother knew before; she had to meet a different person," Sonia says.

That is when the abuse started, and it continued through most of her childhood, tapering off during her high school years. As the oldest of four, Sonia often took the brunt of the abuse and witnessed her mother suffering as well. This unfortunately is a true story for many whose lives have been impacted by an alcoholic and how the disease can spiral into violence and abuse of the mother and children.

"I feel it is important for me to help people understand that, at the very basic foundation, we need to make others aware of domestic violence and raise awareness that this can happen to anyone," says Sonia.

In 2009, she put her passion to action. She remembers, "While standing in one of the original domestic violence shelters of our great city, a second-year medical student looked at me imploringly and asked, 'Is this where people live?' It was a question that I had not wanted to ask myself. My mind had not been reflective, it was hurried. And, in my hurry to teach this wonderful student, the realization was barely sinking in, that a mother was sleeping in this shelter with her children."

To convert these shelters into havens would become her mission. She wondered, "How?" and realized, "Quite simply, it takes a village." She set out to gather members of her community, her family, and friends, knowing intuitively that, to sustain the mission, "a village would be critical."

Sonia hopes that society will start shifting its perceptions about domestic violence and that people will stand up and speak up, taking away the power of its secrecy. "It's nothing to be ashamed about. If we keep feeling ashamed and keep this issue a secret, we will forever be trapped."

In a letter to Be Alright volunteers, she wrote: "Every time you participate in a Be Alright event, we are that much closer to creating a world where violence is no longer tolerated and where decisions are not reactive but mindful. You are shaping a world of peace and understanding."

GRATEFUL LIFE PRACTICE

As a physician, Sonia feels strongly that her role is to educate the medical residents she teaches to be aware of the signs of domestic violence, and to that end she weaves her personal and professional mission into her daily life as her gratitude practice. She includes these resources that she believes are important to share with others.

- Connections for Abused Women and Their Children (CAWC): www.cawc.org
- The National Domestic Violence Hotline: www.thehotline.org

- Illinois Coalition Against Domestic Violence: www.ilcadv.org
- Break the Cycle: www.breakthecycle.org

Find more information on Be Alright on her website: sites.google.com/site/bealrightchicago.

AFTER CANCER, GRATITUDE FOR BLESSINGS

Illness is part of a larger human tradition of initiation, an opportunity in life which is present for us all. As I understand it, initiation is a time when a shift in consciousness occurs and a new path opens for us. And while nothing has changed, everything is different. We see the same world differently. It is a profound personal transformation of experience.

—Rachel Naomi Remen, M.D.,
author, pioneer of integrative medicine, and co-founder and
medical director of the Commonweal Cancer Help Program

On a beautiful spring day in 2010, Eileen Timmins learned that her journey in life would include experiencing breast cancer. Receiving the news, the then high-powered HR exec felt as if the familiar had fallen away. But at the same time, it was as if a new door had opened.

During her treatment at Northwestern Memorial Hospital in Chicago, Eileen also discovered a labyrinth in the courtyard of nearby St. James Cathedral. As her external blueprint was becoming fuzzy, Eileen began to follow an inner compass and take risks that were unthinkable before. Through what she dubs her "dis-ease," Eileen developed a greater trust in life than before, a deeper faith, and a greater sense of what really mattered.

Walks in the labyrinth led to a path of initiation opening for Eileen, like the one Dr. Remen describes. Like the ancient and mysterious circular path of a labyrinth that curves back upon itself, her personal journey was not a straight one. It was winding inward toward her inner essence and toward healing.

" 'Walking it' had a huge impact on my healing," she says.

After six months of treatment, moments of profound and enduring change emerged. Eileen saw for the first time what her soul had always known. Forgiveness was the emotion consistently appearing to her in many forms during the beginning of her journey. She embarked on her own transformational and healing journey to release wrongs, including "The wrongs that I held against myself, the wrongs inflicted upon me from others, and wrongs I inflicted upon others."

"By forgiving, you are releasing the initial harm," she says. "The real gift comes from releasing the second harm, the energy you have been using to hold on to it. By releasing the second harm, you are releasing them / it from your present and your future.

"After experiencing a 'dis-ease' and understanding that I too was one who was not forgiving, I performed some soul-searching and research to realize my disease had much to do with emotions. My passion to spread the word on the process of forgiveness began." She wrote the book The Forgiveness Fairy: Sharing the Light of Forgiveness and founded Aingilin (which means "little angel" in Gaelic) with a mission "to create a better future for the world through acts of service." She spends her days as a human resources consultant. Additionally, she is an adjunct professor at DePaul University and serves on multiple boards. Eileen is a motivational speaker, leadership expert, coach, board member, professor, author, artist, and labyrinth builder. She says she is on a mission to shift the energy of the world by one forgiving act at a time.

Hers isn't a story of pain and suffering. It is a story about a shift, a huge personal awakening. It is about resilience and change, and the power of love and forgiveness to heal physically, emotionally, and spiritually with grace.

And it is an experience that became an occasion of gratitude, a realization that, from all that was lost, something of great value was found. During the course of her treatment, Eileen constantly expressed her appreciation for the nurses, doctors, techs, and other healthcare providers working to help her heal. Just before she was being transported to a treatment or consulting about test results, she would hand them thank-you cards with gift cards, saying, "Have a tea on me."

"I didn't want to be treated differently," she says, "but I wanted everything to be positive, to have them *help me move forward to release these fears, past hurts, resentments, anger, and judgments. I thanked them for helping me."*

Way before experiencing cancer in her life, Eileen learned the lesson about making space for blessings that were circling around her life waiting for her attention in the midst of challenges that seemed to surround her. Who would know that she was being schooled all along for the very moment of her diagnosis? She describes her life as one of "change and resilience."

Born the second to the youngest of five to first generation of Irish immigrants, her parents, Martin and Marianne, the family lived in the Bronx. That was until one day in the early 1970s when en route to work as an associate at Met Life, Eileen's dad witnessed a stabbing on the subway. He decided the crime-ridden streets of New York City weren't where he wanted to raise his children. Enrolled in night school to become a lawyer, thanks to the GI Bill and in pursuit of a great job opportunity, her dad loaded up the station wagon and moved the clan to Waunakee, WI, a small village of about 2,000 at the time outside of Madison, and worlds away from The Big Apple.

The land of dairy farms seemed the perfect place to raise a family. What more could the Timmins family ask for? But the transition wasn't so flawless for seven-year-old Eileen, who was struggling with a stutter and attended speech therapy. It was hard at first to fit in with the other kids.

The rural countryside turned into a scary place one day when Eileen, then 17, was driving with a friend and came across a horrific accident. A drunk driver, a kid coming out of a bar and driving a truck, had smashed into the station wagon Eileen's mom and dad were driving while coming home from Christmas shopping. Eileen arrived at the accident to hear her dad screaming, "My wife, my wife!" as the county sheriffs were loading her parents into an ambulance. The officer would not let Eileen get in with them, and she remembers punching him, then running down the road along the cornfields, crying and chasing the ambulance. A passerby stopped (it turned out he, coincidentally, was a Rotary Club member who knew her dad) and drove her to the hospital. "Mr. Mohs drove into a cornfield, damaged his car, and cautiously drove me to the hospital to be with my parents," says Eileen. Later, Eileen would have the chance to thank this gentleman for his act of kindness.

Her mother was so severely injured that doctors later told Eileen it was a miracle she lived. But, they recounted that the grace and providence that stepped in, when Eileen just happened to drive up to the scene of the accident and be present for her mother, gave her mother the will to live. Eileen believes an angel was present to assist in this energy of life.

Life pushed forward. After an unhealthy and abusive relationship, Eileen met the love of her life, Bill Schick, a former NFL football player who was working as a lineman coach at the University of Wisconsin. At the time, Eileen was working as an executive assistant and going to night school to pursue what turned out to be several degrees, leading years later to her Ph.D. in organizational development and human resources. Boardroom bound, her resume reads like an entry in *Who's Who*, with executive vice president positions and board posts at some of Chicago's leading firms.

Fast-forward to 1992, when the couple had moved to Chicago and were living a happy life, both successful in their careers. One night, their cab driver spun out of control and smashed into a steak house in the heart of Chicago's popular Gold Coast district. The impact propelled Eileen through the windshield, leaving her with broken bones and PTSD flashbacks of her parents' accident.

In 2000, Eileen's mother was diagnosed with breast cancer. Her strong Irish spirit and positive attitude led to a recovery, which lasted a few years. But in 2004, just after she and her husband celebrated their 50th anniversary, Eileen's mom shared with the family that the cancer had reoccurred. This time around, it was time for her to "go to the other side." God needed her now. She passed away in August of 2005.

Eileen would keep moving forward, working hard on

her dissertation for her Ph.D. and on breaking through the glass ceiling in the male-dominated industry. "At one point, I just wanted to pinch myself, I felt so blessed."

In 2010, she discovered a lump in her breast. Determined not to get sucked into the amnesia of sickness and to let the experience of cancer consume her body and soul, Eileen began her inward journey. She says she realized: "I had not been taking care of myself. I had been shutting my life out, keeping busy and working constantly to block the hurts and to not feel the grief.

"It was a huge awakening," she recalls. She did what she was best at in her career: She researched intensely the specifics of her cancer. That's when she discovered the pivotal role that emotions like anger and resentment play in feeding the "dis-ease" and experience of cancer.

Eileen discovered that gratitude is an antidote to the dis-ease she was experiencing, and that what whispers to some that they are NOT at ease is what disease truly means. She started seeing in Technicolor the blessings that were hovering all around her. One was her friend Franchee who also was facing the challenge of cancer. "She helped me through all the treatments and did so well during her own chemo and radiation. We grew very close during this time together."

In the end, Franchee displayed "so much courage." What turned into an epiphany for Eileen was that Franchee forgave all the people—and herself—before she passed away. Eileen observed this when her mother died too. Loud and clear, a message was sent to Eileen to share the acts of how to forgive. Why wait to forgive? Do it now.

"My goal became to help carry on her message," says Eileen. There are of course the obvious places to share the message of forgiveness—friends, family, and others—but Eileen feels strongly that it needs to be shared in boardrooms, to corporate leaders to end grudges, resentments, manipulation, and blame. She knows that authentic leaders aren't about greed but are about forgiveness. It is about facing the issue, moving on, and learning from it. It is a message she brings to her students as an adjunct professor at DePaul University, and one she is seeking to explore at a new level.

In the meantime, Eileen believes the experience of cancer was a positive shift, and is focusing on paying close attention to the movement of grace and gratitude in her life.

These days she's showing her gratitude with a labyrinth she helped fund and build that is open to the public on her sister's farm, Hillsong Ridge, near Madison, Wisconsin, modeled after a pattern built into the floor of Chartres Cathedral in France dating back to 1201. Walkers follow a compact series of switchbacks to a center signifying love, surrounded by a rosette pattern with six petals symbolizing faith, surrender, service, abundance, forgiveness, and overcoming.

THIS IS THE POEM EILEEN WROTE AND LIVES BY:

When by opening fully to our own experience we can
  feel and see the resilience of life around us...,
In the caterpillar that develops wings
In the small bird that is learning to fly
In the rose bud that is opening
Flow like water
Bend like a branch
Accept it with Grace
Move and grow
Learn and become new.

GRATEFUL LIFE PRACTICE

Upon awakening each day Eileen prays, mediates, and recites her affirmations.

She prays:

To the Holy Spirit and Mary, Mother of God, to protect her and send only loving energies to and from her each day,

To Archangel Raphael to infuse her with his green healing energy,

To Archangel Michael to protect her with his energy.

Meditation includes asking the angels, "What do you want to share with me today?" This is also performed in the evening before she goes to bed: Angels, what message do you want me to remember from my dreams?

She voices affirmations of gratitude every day and night to keep herself balanced and "to continually send love and many blessings to all—remembering we are all connected."

CHAPTER FIVE

HOW GRATITUDE TURNS WHAT WE HAVE IN OUR LIVES INTO ENOUGH—AND MORE

Expect something good to happen to you no matter what occurred yesterday. Realize the past no longer holds you captive. It can only continue to hurt you if you hold on to it. Let the past go. A simply abundant world awaits.

—Sarah Ban Breathnach,
Simple Abundance: A Daybook of Comfort and Joy

If there is one thing that is certain in life it is this: its impermanence and uncertainty.

With that comes the reality that life can deal some tough blows: Your job and financial security are suddenly pulled like a rug from under you; a flood or natural disaster sweeps away your home and the physical foundation of your life; a loved one is ill or suffering. The list can go on.

But there are certain people who have an ability to focus on the sweet in the middle of the bitter. In bad times and good, they demonstrate a resiliency of the human spirit that leaves many of us gaping in awe. How do they turn grief and pain into compassion for others? What important lessons do they have to teach all of us about living fully even in the difficult moments that we hope will pass quickly? How can we learn to tap into the sense of confidence that, even in times of harm and suffering, seems to be instilled in them?

You can do this too. The secret lies in cultivating gratitude as a powerful tool for overcoming adversity and depression. When we choose to focus on our blessings, rather than whining or obsessing about life's hard knocks, we nourish good feelings about ourselves and others. We find an inner source of resilience and happiness buried underneath the yucky circumstances.

One caveat: This doesn't happen overnight. You need to take gradual steps. Gratitude is habit-forming. When life is stressful, slow down. In this chapter, we investigate what propels some people to uncover stars shining in the rubble of destruction. Gratefulness seems to be their middle name. We're not Pollyannas, so we reached out to these grateful sojourners to see how focusing on their blessings lifts the malaise.

One thing that they all agreed on is that giving thanks for all that happens—good or bad—strengthens your relationship with spirit and how spiritual prosperity manifests itself in the world. Realizing that connection to spirit helps us see that good things abound, even when it's really hard to dig through to find them. When we view our lives in this way, we see how fortunate we are each and every day.

A FLOOD OF GRATITUDE FOR FRIENDS
WHO BECAME FIRST RESPONDERS:
HARDSHIP BRINGS A COMMUNITY OF CARING
AND GENEROSITY

Life isn't about waiting for the storm to pass, it's about learning to dance in the rain.

—*Vivian Greene*

Jeff and KC Faetz bolted awake about four a.m. on Wednesday, June 26, 2013, in a panic. The heavy rains and winds outside flashed them back to the flood three years earlier when they lost two cars. They knew they had to hurry, so they scrambled to move their cars to higher ground.

They returned to start placing sandbags around their home. But their efforts were futile, as a wall of water rushed through a basement window of their tri-level home and within five minutes rose 12 feet to the rafters, flooding upward through their family room and rising to the kitchen and living room levels of their Lake Zurich, Illinois, home.

After grabbing what they could, it was clear they had to leave immediately, when firefighters pulled up in a rescue boat and told the couple to evacuate the neighborhood. The village would later be declared the hardest hit by the worst flood in 200 years that dumped 6.6 inches of rain in less than three hours on this suburb 40 miles northwest of Chicago.

The Faetzes had no idea when they would be able to return. Their back and front yards had become a lake. Over the next several days there were a lot of tears, but also gratitude, as family, friends, and strangers arrived en masse and charged full force through the rubble. Most of the possessions of KC, Jeff, and their two college-age sons—Kevin, 22, and Ryan, 21—were later laid out in more than 100 black plastic bags filling their front and back yard.

What was most surprising to this crew of helpers were the words they kept hearing KC saying: "I'm so blessed to have all of these angels." While many would have sunk into a world of grief and emotional despair, KC instinctively navigated the trauma with a practical task focus and an energy of thankfulness as her internal compass to move forward.

Here, KC shares the six months since the flood and her gratefulness for the circle of "angels" who she says

have helped her family push through and forge ahead to
rebuild their lives.

A note sent to KC from her cousins, which she kept on her nightstand, became her mantra: "Together we are stronger than any flood waters."

The depth of their loss quickly became apparent: Jeff's home office, including all his computer, video, and filming equipment was destroyed, not to mention the technology and tools needed to pursue his vocation, avocation, and joy of filming. The basement and family room level were destroyed, along with most of the family's Christmas treasures, baseball and train collections, and all their electronics, including their heater, air conditioners, washing machine, etc.

At the same time there were other challenges. Jeff was still regaining full health following a stroke he had suffered months before, and KC's especially close uncle and mentor was diagnosed with cancer that would take his life just months after the flood. Meantime, during the months following the flood, KC started feeling ill, and lost 30 pounds. "I just kept thinking it was because of the stress," she says. But after undergoing a battery of tests, she was diagnosed with polymyalgia rheumatica, an inflammatory disorder that causes muscle pain and stiffness.

During the cleanup, the insurance investigators arrived to say sump pump coverage was denied because backup water was "co-mingling with flood waters."

"So much of our lives was coming out in big black garbage bags," KC remembers, describing the days that followed. "I just remember feeling so overwhelmed and I really don't even remember Thursday, the day after the flood. I just looked at all those bags, and for every bag I cleaned out, another five would be waiting."

By Friday, a troop of friends—and people she had barely known—started appearing, digging in deeper than KC says she ever could. Another neighbor, a recent widow, also welcomed KC and Jeff into her home to live during the week that the village quarantined their house. (The boys were away at college, which KC says she was "very grateful for so I could focus on the fixing of what needed to be done, like sump pump shopping and details of restoring our home.") Ground Zero became the home of another set of friends, Theresa and Pat and their three teenaged children, who were omnipresent, moving collectibles and boxes to be stored in their basement and working for the months that followed on the carpentry, taping, and rebuilding of the Faetzes' home. KC's brother-in-law Dan worked with neighbor Pat for months to do home repairs.

Some friends took treasures and loads of laundry home to wash and restore—28 years of family photo albums, Christmas stockings, Jeff's extensive collection of baseball cards, the Lionel train sets handed down to Jeff by his family. "One woman I knew only very casually from a golf class I took walked by the house and pitched in with a labor of love," KC recalls. Others rolled up their sleeves and cleaned floors and washed down the Christmas ornaments, and started washing down everything laid out across the backyard.

Restaurant owners from Lake Zurich set up a way station down the street to provide food and water for KC and the owners of 17 other houses that had been hit by the flood. KC's was the most devastated because of the water that rushed through the windows and flooded her home from the basement upwards. Cars driven by townsfolk, friends, and others she had never met drove by with trays of food and bottled water.

One woman, the mother of one of Kevin's friends, drove by and handed KC $500 in an envelope, saying, "Someone once helped me and I want to pay it forward and help you." Another couple, friends, arrived at Paddy's on the Square, an Irish boutique where KC works part-time, with an envelope containing $500 to help cover replacement costs. A representative from a local church, Alpine Chapel, arrived to ask, "What can we do to help? Do you need a team of us to help clean? What can we do?" Early the next week they showed up with a water heater and installed it.

A month after the flood, a group of friends rallied to stage a surprise fund-raiser for KC and Jeff at their favorite pub, the Island, in Libertyville.

Indeed, it wasn't the story of loss so much as the generosity and gratitude that truly reflect the scope of devastation, and the tenacity of spirit that fueled KC and her family.

"There were so, so many blessings," says KC. "Like the fact that we knew to save our cars, and the friends who showed up immediately and did whatever they could. It's one thing to have people donate time, or to have them help with the financial costs, but I had a trifecta: angels who donated their time, shared their energy, and helped us financially. Looking back reminds me of how far we have come and how many people were there for us."

Today, KC is thankful and looking forward. In the aftermath of all the devastation, she has found a place inside herself, untouched by the flood, a place that is her anchor and her true home, regardless of what happened to her actual house. It's the place that was held afloat by the love of family and friends.

"When I think about all that everyone did," she says, "I am amazed at all their strength and selflessness. It was a very scary day, and the actions of these people helped in keeping my family safe, and for that we are forever grateful. My family was wonderful," she adds. "I grew up with such a small one, but after the flood, I feel my family is huge. As hard as it was to thank all for everything, I have learned to say 'I love you' a bit better. It was something I wasn't good at."

GRATEFUL LIFE PRACTICE

After the flood, KC's mother suggested that she keep a journal by her bedside and write down a blessing that happened each day. She always starts with, "My mom woke up today," as she knows how blessed she is to have a mom who is 88 and lives fully independent and in good health.

TIPS FOR BEING GRATEFUL IN THE MIDST OF PHYSICAL OR EMOTIONAL PAIN

- Don't let your pain stop you from following your heart's desires and passions.
- Be open to reinvention as you adjust to your "new normal."
- Remember that pain and suffering, if you survive it, will make you much stronger and wiser, with many more gifts to give to the world.
- Don't settle, don't stop believing in yourself. You're the most important person in the world.
- Give to others. I guarantee it will help you immensely.
- Don't focus on the negative. It makes you bitter and draws away essential energies that you need elsewhere.
- Practice appreciation throughout the day.
- Forgive the person or people you are angry at. When you forgive, you send out positive energies and that has a ripple effect.

EVERY PARENT'S WORST NIGHTMARE:
HOW GRATITUDE AND STORYTELLING HELPED
A FAMILY PERSEVERE AND ASSIST OTHERS

Grief can be the garden of compassion. If you keep your heart open through everything, your pain can become your greatest ally in your life's search for love and wisdom.

—*Rumi*

Monica Wesolowska's first son, Silvan, was born April 27, 2003, in a Berkeley, California, hospital after a normal pregnancy and seemingly routine labor and delivery. A few hours after his birth, however, Silvan began to have seizures. After days of testing, Monica and her husband learned that their beautiful boy had suffered severe and irreparable brain damage sometime during birth. "We already love him," she writes in her memoir Holding Silvan: A Brief Life. *"We love him as a newborn, his loamy-scented head, the soft heft of his thighs, the tiny thump of the heart in his chest... Since he came into the*

world through love, since he's been surrounded by it, I'd
like him to leave knowing nothing else but love...."

It was out of this immense devotion that Wesolowska
and her husband decided not to feed Silvan, and to let him
die. In her beautifully written book, we learn how Monica's love for her son empowered her to fight for his right to
die, and how this heartbreaking experience was ultimately
life-affirming. Monica's transformative memoir details
the process of letting go, yet she holds onto her grateful
attitude. How is this humanly possible? In an interview,
she reveals what kept her afloat when others might have
drowned in grief and bitterness.

"Loss is easier to bear when you have fully loved," said
Monica Wesolowska, which is perhaps the greatest lesson
we can learn about living a life without regrets. Monica
and her husband held their son every day as they watched
his infant body wither, and theirs is a story that teaches us
about the deepest reaches of love.

Fortunately, the ethics committee at their hospital—
including doctors, nurses, social workers, legal counsel,
and laypeople—agreed with their decision to let their
son die. She recounts that they said, "Usually parents
come to us with the opposite request, wanting to go to
such extremes to save their children that we don't feel it's
compassionate. What you are doing is rare, but we recognize that it's coming from love."

But once he was gone, how was Monica able to recover and persevere?

She explains that "there must be a natural coping mechanism for many in crisis, but it is in the aftermath that people diverge the most." Her story sheds light on what qualities help people work through loss and find hope at the other end. One of them is a sense of gratitude. She says that, throughout their experience, she and her husband recounted the ways in which they were lucky. "Isn't it lucky we live so close to the hospital?" "Aren't we lucky we have insurance?" and "We are so lucky we don't have to go to work but can spend all our time with Silvan."

Today, Monica, her husband, and two sons who were born after Silvan have a weekly gratitude practice in their home in Berkeley, California. Every Friday evening, they have a ceremony where they each recite what they are grateful for. She says that this spills out to the rest of the week.

Monica also credits her writer-brain for bolstering her coping skills. "Maybe because I am a writer, I am able to hold two contradictory thoughts in my head simultaneously," she says. "For instance: No child is replaceable, and you will never get over losing him or her. However you *will* recover and your life will once again feel full." She counsels the many people she meets who have experienced losing a loved one with that message of hope. Being a writer means she is a storyteller, but even if you don't craft sentences for a living, that activity can be invaluable, she says.

Thankfully, she says, she had people who would listen.

"My friends were willing to listen in depth, over a year, to what we were experiencing. It felt wrong to be silent, and so I talked about Silvan all the time, and this helped me to heal." Her husband, David, had his own need to heal, and being able to talk about Silvan was a crucial part of that process. "After two months, when David returned to work, his boss, trying to be helpful, sent out a company-wide e-mail welcoming David back, and asked people not to bring up the subject of Silvan." David, a computer programmer, soon found that was untenable, and he too began to talk to his co-workers.

Being a writer and storyteller, Monica is also a "big listener." This enables her to realize that everyone has a story, which in turn supports her naturally compassionate nature.

She also counsels families in similar situations to live in the moment, love fully, and then let go. She says she feels "lucky" that she was able to do that, but understands how culturally ingrained it is to withdraw. "A woman at work came to me shortly after Silvan died to tell me that her daughter had a baby who was going to die. She was very upset because her daughter loved this baby so much. My co-worker was trying to persuade her daughter to leave the baby at the hospital to die so that she wouldn't 'bond' with it," Monica says. "She told me she wasn't going to meet her grandchild because she thought this would make the loss easier. I urged her to go and meet her grandchild. I told her this would make her feel better. She followed through and was glad she did."

Monica thinks there is a cultural shift taking place, a shift for the better. In the not-too-distant past, if a baby was terribly deformed, for instance, doctors would tell the parents their baby didn't make it, and then let the baby die. The parents weren't given a choice about whether they could even meet their babies. Today, if a baby is stillborn, for example, it's acceptable for the mother and father to be given a meaningful moment with their child before they let go.

Today, immersed in her very busy life as a writer, teacher, and mother of two young sons, Monica still takes the time to speak to hospitals about her experience, and talk one-on-one with anyone who has lost a newborn. She says she is not so different than she has always been—she has always preferred to have intimate conversations—but today those conversations help her overcome day-to-day annoyances by reminding her that "the person who cut me off in traffic may have been rushing to the hospital, as I once was," and it also helps her to continue holding her son, "holding Silvan" in her heart and memory for as long as she lives.

GRATEFUL LIFE PRACTICE

If you have lost someone dear to you, as so many of us have, give yourself time. Understand that the way grief is experienced is unique, and that your journey through bereavement is entirely personal to you. So many people who have navigated the dying and grieving process find that embracing and practicing gratitude gives them the opportunity to acknowledge the death of their beloved and eventually move forward with the knowledge that their memories are blessings. As Robin Gaphni states in her blog, griefgratitude.com, "By acknowledging and appreciating life's impermanence, I am left with deep gratitude for what is right now."

COUNTING THEIR BLESSINGS: BEST FRIENDS CELEBRATE CALL TO CARE FOR THEIR MOTHERS

Sometimes I need only to stand wherever I am to be blessed.

—Mary Oliver

Longtime friends Andrea Hurley and Judy Fox share a lot in common. They met more than 25 years ago through their dual interest in spiritual depth and meditation. Both have pursued entrepreneurial professions. Andrea lives in the Boston area with her husband and child and owns her own web design firm, Elytra Design. Judy, single, is an artist who lives in Lenox, Massachusetts, and is currently staying in Florida to care for her mother, along with a professional caregiver.

Almost overnight, the close friends found themselves thrust into a new role, caring for their aging moms, joining the ranks of almost 45 million baby boomers who are primary caregivers for their aging parents.

Judy's mom, Selma Fox, is almost 98, and Andrea's mom, Rita Hurley, is 95. What Judy and Andrea also share is a belief that caregiving is a role they were called to and a commitment that they would be present for during their moms' final and precious years. The thought that their moms would experience these years alone was unbearable.

In addition, they share the belief that caregiving is a gift. They are grateful for the opportunity to spend the days and moments alongside their moms at this stage when they need their daughters to care.

"Living as I do most of the time now with my mom, gratitude takes on even more significance," says Judy. "Every drop of goodness that my mom expresses, experiences, and responds to, and every drop of goodness that I experience with her and with others is treasured. I am filled with gratitude and a quiet happiness—goodness abounds and life is full."

They also realized that the odds are many fellow baby boomer folks experiencing this turning table might benefit from the conversations, support, and friendship Judy and Andrea pledged to share as they formed a circle of support around their moms. Believing that stories are a powerful vehicle to help others know they are not alone, Judy and Andrea launched the blog

"When the Table Turns" (www.whenthetableturns. com) where they share their philosophical and heartfelt reflections and experiences on the frontline of caring for their moms.

We asked the friends to share their reflections on the gratitude and the blessings they say they are experiencing daily since they have accepted "the call" to accompany their 90-something moms through their final years.

JUDY FOX: ON CARING FOR HER MOM, SELMA FOX

Judy's mom, 97, was living independently, cooking, and driving; she was playing bridge until she was 93. Judy would go to Florida to visit her twice a year, and her mom would visit her in Lenox, Massachusetts. But gradually it became obvious that the independence was slipping away.

"More and more I was in contact with her, calling her on the phone daily, and then, on one visit about five years ago, she was very weak and became hospitalized with a restricted aortic valve. Everything radically changed, and we had to hire a professional aide to be with her. We were lucky because Pat (the caregiver) had taken care of my aunt, who had Parkinson's, for 11 years, so she was like a family member."

After that, Judy started to be with her mom more and more—at first about 50 percent of the time, and then it gradually increased. "I was thrust into ongoing doctors' appointments and different treatment possibilities, which meant I had to investigate for myself the various options. We ended up going down to Cali, Columbia, where my mom had an aortic valve replacement via a catheter, which at that time was not FDA-approved in the USA. It was incredibly courageous of my mom to make the trip, as it was not a given she would survive, but she said to me, 'What choice do I have?' And it was a success."

Then, 15 months ago, Judy's mom had a stroke and was paralyzed on her left side. At that point, there was no other option than for Judy to move down to Florida with her. She says, "It really is a labor of love. I am the only close family member, as my brother and father died many years ago and my mother was the youngest in the family and the only one left now. It has never been a chore to be with my mom—definitely not always easy, but I had absolutely no ambivalence when I decided to be with her—it was almost a choice-less decision and continues to be choice-less. It's the heart's response to love."

Today, Judy says she feels her whole life was leading up to the moment when she would walk with her mom through this journey. "I can experience this gratitude on a daily basis. I am at that point where I am no longer seeing life through the narcissistic lens of what life has to give to me. It's in part a result of getting older and maturing, having had a lot of life and death experience and a long history of spiritual practice in many forms, including meditation."

The experience reinforces her belief that going through difficult times is a catalyst for gratitude.

"I have also always been a very reflective and sensitive person, with a desire to touch upon the essentials in life, to evolve and transform," she says. "I also think when one has gone through difficulties in life—the loss of loved ones, sickness of oneself or others, suffering—in a way there are only two choices: either to be a victim of circumstances, to be taken down by them, or to rise up and be triumphant in the best sense of that word."

She adds, "Interestingly, going through difficulties can highlight gratitude as one becomes more attuned and sensitive to those moments, times, days, when the light shines through in all sorts of ways. This has been my experience in helping to look after my mom for the last four-plus years. There is a deepening appreciation for what is truly important. I find I can't take life, goodness, human kindness, moments of genuine connection for granted as I might have done when I was younger."

The slowing down and stripping away of all the other non-essentials also has helped inspire more gratitude in her life, says Judy.

"I have by necessity also been forced to slow down, to become more attentive, more sensitive to my mom and her whole situation and that helps a lot to allow gratitude to flower," she says. "I am living close to death all the time with my mom as she approaches her 98th birthday and that also can put everything into a very big perspective. There is no time for self-concern or worry about small details. As they colloquially say, 'Life is too short.' "

WHERE JUDY FINDS GRATITUDE IN CARING
The Gift of Presence
"I am grateful to actually still have my mom in these later years and to have developed a relationship with her that would probably not have been possible when I was younger. She was different and so was I—she has softened and so have I—and there is so much love and sweetness between us that will stay with me forever."

The Gift of a Just Being
Living with her mother has slowed down Judy's life. "Having more time to reflect and write, I also find I have the chance to appreciate my mother, who she is and was, in a way that I might not have. I would have missed a lot by not being here with her. For example, I appreciate how she has surrendered in such a beautiful way to a less than wonderful situation. Not being able to walk, having very little energy, unable to see much—she is unusually good-spirited most of the time. She fundamentally doesn't complain. She was such a doer, and now when she can't do very much, she still gives so much. I still feel her strength in a different way, I'm inspired by her, and I know this is affecting how I am now and how I will be in the future."

The Gift of Peace

"Since I have been through some major traumas with her, like a stroke, like the immediate need for a pacemaker and the need for an aortic valve replacement, as well as all the small disruptions like infections and colds, I am grateful when there is a calm between the storms, so to speak. I am grateful for the absence of drama and trauma that is definitely part of my caregiving experience in living with her."

The Gift of the Unexpected

"I am grateful for the unexpected—that the day doesn't always follow the night, and that life really does change. Even when things have looked very gloomy, what I have found and am so grateful for is that there is always 'another day' or another moment when things really do change, when my mom changes. For example, for a little while my mother seemed depressed, and then her spirits lifted, seemingly out of the blue, and she was fine, her sense of humor intact. This change has happened in so many ways—sometimes it might come with an unexpected visitor, and sometimes it happens more mysteriously, but it is always greeted with gratitude."

The Gift of Special Moments

"I am grateful for the moments that we share together—listening to her favorite CD, *Kisses on the Bottom*, old-fashioned songs by Paul McCartney, which she loves so much—the times when we just talk together about nothing in particular, or about matters more pointed and poignant, and anything in between. And I am so grateful when we just laugh together and snuggle in her narrow hospital bed."

The Gift of Accepting Help

Lastly, Judy says she is grateful for the professional caregivers who are "loving, human, and funny, and who really do care and appreciate her and thus make it possible for me to be relaxed and unself-conscious." She adds, "I can be myself with them and with my mom and never feel like I am with 'strangers.' As time goes by, I feel more and more gratitude for them and how much they give."

GRATEFUL LIFE PRACTICE

Writing for the blog also gives Judy the space to reflect and slow down. "It gives me that space to communicate with myself and others and bring more light upon whatever is going on. I am deeply grateful for this 'practice,' which in a sense transforms whatever is happening to a higher plane."

ANDREA HURLEY: ON CARING FOR HER MOM, RITA HURLEY

Andrea's mother, now 95, lives in an assisted living facility near Andrea in the Boston area. When Andrea saw that her mother was no longer able to take care of herself, she worried and thought about her all the time. She says, "It wouldn't let go of me and it was painful to see how she was falling into a pattern that many elderly fall into: not eating well, lacking engagement, feeling lonely, and relying on alcohol to relieve her boredom. I knew something had to be done."

At first Andrea looked outside for someone to help, until that day when she realized that person was her. "From that moment on," she says, "I found an incredible peace inside. This surprised me. The burden lifted, but at the same time a new whirlwind entered my life. Many people warned me that this would be a burden, or not to get my hopes up. But something inside me shifted and new perceptions were opening up."

Andrea grew up the seventh of nine kids in an Irish Catholic family from Boston. "My mother made many sacrifices to raise us," she recalls. "She didn't have a career or work-life outside of raising us. I always had a soft spot in my heart for her, and what she gave up for us. My dad died when she was 58, and she has spent many years as a widow caring for my brother, who had a mental illness. When she became elderly I wanted her life story to be acknowledged. I felt it was important."

From an early age, Andrea says gratitude has played a central role in her life. But now it plays a particular role in caring for her elderly mom and in writing the blog with Judy to share their experiences caring for elderly parents.

"As my mother became older and more vulnerable and dependent, I noticed something surprising in the experience of caring for her," says Andrea. "I noticed that my heart was full, content, and pouring with gratitude a lot of the time. This was not something that I willed or made an effort to experience. It was just there, as part of the caregiving experience. And it was surprising because I didn't expect it."

Part of the surprise in experiencing gratitude in her caregiving was because cultural stereotypes present predominately negative perceptions about what caring for an elderly loved one is all about.

At the Heart of Caregiving: Gratitude

"So much of the narrative around caring for our elderly is geared toward stories of burden, stress, and frustration," says Andrea. "Basically negatives. Those experiences are of course real, and I would never pretend otherwise, but I stumbled upon a deeper source of strength as well. It was a quiet place inside that was free of problem, burden, and frustration. I started to pay attention to this dimension of my experience as I cared for my elderly mother, and began to notice that at the heart of this quiet place was gratitude. As I paid attention to it, it seemed to grow of its own accord and fill me with a strength I didn't know I had."

Andrea's mother was close to 90 years old when she and her family began to wake up to noticeable changes in her. She was living alone, not eating so well, taking a few too many drinks, and her memory was slipping, says Andrea. Her personality was getting more rigid, and their conversations were more like a broken record. "I felt my mother needed more of her kids, more time with us," she remembers. "She needed more engagement. She needed a big huge dose of love regularly infused into her life. But her kids have full-time jobs, with kids and grandkids of our own. We have busy lives that are already hard to manage. Our full lives did not make it possible to be with my mother 24/7, which is what she really needed. We did what we could, or even more than we could, to keep her from slipping further away."

The Summer of Gratitude

Then came the summer of 2011, "which was the most trying summer of my life on one hand, and on the other it was the summer of gratitude," says Andrea.

She explains: "My mother was 93 years old. She was making her annual migration to the Adirondacks in New York to spend her summer on a lake in our big, old, friendly family cottage of over 60 years. It is a charming cottage, with five bedrooms, requiring an ascent up 14 very steep stairs to go to bed at night. My mother had spent all her summers there since the early 1950s (along with my dad when he was alive). And so this year, just like every other year, she packed her small suitcase, and asked if someone could drive her there from her home in Massachusetts.

(This was the first summer since she had given up driving.) Lovingly and willingly, one of my sisters jumped at the opportunity to take her. I, on the other hand, panicked. "No! She can't be alone! We didn't find anyone to take care of her yet! This is all happening too fast! The stairs!" But it was too late. Off she went to the lake."

In those panic-stricken moments, Andrea thought hard and deep, searching for who could help. "And then, in an unexpected moment, I looked at my life and saw that I could do it," she says. "I could leave home for the summer, pack up my office, work from the cottage, and take care of her." Within three days, Andrea was driving to the Adirondacks, "with my files and my computer and a surprising degree of calm in my heart. That was the beginning of a flowering of gratitude that took me by surprise."

Fast forward to July 28, 2011, 10 p.m. "I had been watching my mother like a hawk for the past month as she hiked up those 14 stairs to her bedroom at night. I would always stay close at hand. And for the whole month, she did remarkably well. I said to one of my siblings just that day, 'Mom is doing great on the stairs, she really is so careful.' So when that night came and she said she was going off to bed, I relaxed my hawk eyes and let her go on her own: 'I'll just check my e-mail, Mom, and will be up to kiss you good night in a couple minutes.' Two minutes later the nightmare happened. The tumble. The scream. It seemed to last forever. By the time I reached her, she was almost at the bottom step. Ninety-three years old. Fourteen stairs. Oh my God, could she survive this?"

Enter Terror. Enter Grace.

Her mother, with her head pouring blood, could still speak to Andrea. She only wanted to go back up the stairs to bed. A neighbor was walking by outside the house and Andrea yelled for help. Within three minutes there were 20 people in the house, several first responders. She says, "Calling the ambulance, calling the rest of my siblings, I stayed locked onto my mother's frightened eyes. All I could see was the flickering of the life force—it could go either way. And through the ambulance ride, one hour to the hospital, all she kept saying was, 'Andrea where are you?' And I would say, 'Right here Mom. I'm right here.' Into the ER, hours of waiting for tests, and then results. Ten staples in her head. The doctors, like angels, didn't bat an eye at that. Her neck still in a brace. Her body still strapped till the results from the CAT scan came in."

Gratitude Praying Through Her

Andrea wasn't meaning to pray, but she remembers that the universe seemed to be praying through her. "Not moving, it was as though I could hear every good intention of everyone who knew my mother. Praying. What will be will be. But if my mother broke her hip or her neck, the quality of her final years would be profoundly changed.

And I knew I would have to live with this, with the knowledge that my family had entrusted me with taking care of my mother, and that, in one moment of not looking, everything changed."

The doctor finally came out to the waiting room. He said, "I have no idea how this was possible. I have never seen a 93-year-old make such a tumble and not break a bone, but there is no evidence of fracture in any of the scans. Your mother must have an angel looking over her."

Andrea remembers, "A silent gratitude filled the room. I looked at my mother, knowing she passed through the eye of a needle. I knew this was a miracle. Maybe my dad, gone now almost 40 years, played a hand in a spiritual way we can't really know with the mind but can intuit in our hearts. Whatever is true, along with the doctors, EMTs, and emergency responders, I give him my thanks for that mysterious unknown factor that not only saved her life that night, but spared her from breaking a single bone."

Since then, Andrea says, gratitude has "filled every cell of my being and given me a strength that I never knew possible. I took care of my mother for the rest of the summer, tended her as she recuperated and regained her strength. We lived in a state of gratitude. Many times a day she would say, "Andrea, what would I do without you?" Her gratitude filled my gratitude. My gratitude filled hers. And out of this gratitude came so much lightness of being, so much joy, and so much understanding. It was as if this gratitude had a life of its own, greeting the day through the morning rays of light, in the sounds of the ripples on the lake, in the music of the wind as it danced through the quaking leaves of the majestic poplar trees, or in the ephemeral appearance of the double rainbow arching over my mother's cottage a few weeks later."

Gratitude, as Andrea has come to see, "is the deepest essence of life itself. It is everywhere, all the time. And when you see this, your life is never the same again. So that is the story of the gratitude that changed my life, saved my mother's life, and is the source, energy, and commitment from where I engage with my mother, now almost 96 years old, and from where I write the blog."

Find more information on the "When the Table Turns" blog at www.whenthetableturns.com.

CHAPTER SIX

A SERVING OF THANKS A DAY KEEPS THE DOCTOR AWAY: SCIENCE SUBSTANTIATES THE HEALTH BENEFITS OF GRATITUDE

Healing is a matter of time, but it is sometimes also a matter of opportunity.

—*Hippocrates*

In this book we hope to inspire others to take up the practice of gratitude because we've found that consistently acknowledging the good in one's life is a surefire way to cultivate contentment and improve physical health.

Imagine how grateful we are that, since the publication of our previous book, *Living Life as a Thank You*, the Greater Good Science Center at the University of California, Berkeley (GGSC), working with leading researchers, continues to stockpile scientific evidence that practicing gratitude has a measurable effect on physical health. The GGSC's trailblazing coverage of the science of gratitude can be accessed through its website, greatergood.berkeley.edu, where you can also sign up to receive the organization's newsletter.

GRATITUDE IS GOOD FOR YOUR HEALTH: EXPERT ADVICE

For each new morning with its light...,
For rest and shelter of the night...,
For health and food, for love and friends,
For everything Thy goodness sends...

—Author Unknown

The Greater Good Science Center's range of study covers many of the subjects we've covered in other chapters—gratitude in the workplace, how gratitude helps to overcome adversity, how grateful people are more altruistic, and much more. So much in fact, that in this chapter we decided to focus on just one area of their research: the effect of gratitude on physical health.

Building on their findings that consciously choosing to focus on the positive can combat the release of stress hormones that compromise our immune systems and cause inflammation and disease, the GGSC is now funding specific studies that have the potential to improve the lives of millions, if not billions, of people worldwide.

In 2011, the Greater Good Science Center—in collaboration with the University of California, Davis—awarded $3 million in grants to expand the scientific understanding of gratitude, supported with funding from the John Templeton Foundation. One of its key goals is to expand the scientific database of gratitude, particularly in the area of health.

According to Emiliana R. Simon-Thomas, Ph.D., the science director of the Greater Good Science Center, who oversees the GGSC's "Expanding Gratitude" project, they received almost 300 applications from institutions across the United States. A neuroscientist who earned her doctorate in cognition, brain, and behavior at UC Berkeley, Dr. Simon-Thomas's research has explored the neuro-biological roots of pro-social emotion and behavior, as well as the psychosocial benefits of emotional authenticity and connection. Before joining the GGSC, she was the Associate Director / Senior Scientist at the Center for Compassion and Altruism Research and Education (CCARE) at Stanford University.

Fourteen awards were given, including one to Naomi Eisenberger, director of the Social and Affective Neuroscience Laboratory at UCLA, for her project titled "Giving Thanks: Is 'Giving' Key to the Health Benefits of

Gratitude?" Dr. Eisenberger's study uses gene expression and brain-scanning measures to examine some of the biological and neural underpinnings of gratitude.

Jeff Huffman, from Harvard Medical School, was awarded a grant for his project titled "The Impact of Gratitude on Biology and Behavior in Persons with Heart Disease," which examines gratitude in people recently suffering a common and prototypical medical event: an acute coronary syndrome (ACS—a heart attack or related condition). By examining links between gratitude, health behaviors, biomarkers, and outcomes, this study will assess the role that gratitude can play in the healing process following an acute illness.

These studies, and others that focus on gratitude and health, will provide empirical data to further our understanding of the connection between positive emotions and well-being.

When we asked Dr. Simon-Thomas to describe how "a serving of gratitude a day helps to keep the doctor away," she described a three-part process that includes savoring the moment, self-transcendence, and the strengthening of connections. "Gratitude melds together savoring, an acknowledgement of something greater than ourselves, and also strengthens the connection between your reward circuitry and social-cognitive processing regions," she explains.

In a GGSC essay, Robert Emmons, perhaps the world's

leading scientific expert on gratitude, expands on the importance of the social dimension as being especially important to gratitude. "I see it as a relationship-strengthening emotion," Emmons writes, "because it requires us to see how we've been supported and affirmed by other people."

Numerous studies have shown the importance of social connections to health and healing. In fact, researchers from Brigham Young University reviewed 148 studies that tracked the social habits of more than 300,000 people. They found that people who have strong ties to family, friends, or co-workers have a 50 percent lower risk of dying over a given period than those with fewer social connections.

And one of the best ways to strengthen your connectivity with others is to give thanks for the role that others play in your life. It's good for your health!

GRATEFUL LIFE PRACTICE
Try incorporating gratitude as a first step in an exercise program. While you are lacing up your running shoes for a trip to the gym, or to ride your bike, or to go to Zumba class, give thanks for your feet, your legs, the tendons that connect them, and the bones that give them structure. Thank yourself for taking care of your body, and acknowledge that saying "thanks" is a form of exercise too—one that has just as many health dividends as your workout!

AGAINST ALL ODDS: THE HEALING POWER OF A CIRCLE OF SUPPORT

In the end, though, maybe we must all give up trying to pay back the people in this world who sustain our lives. In the end, maybe it's wiser to surrender before the miraculous scope of human generosity and to just keep saying thank you, forever and sincerely, for as long as we have voices.

—Elizabeth Gilbert

It was Halloween in 1995 when Gloria Linn, then 39, a first-grade teacher at a Navajo reservation from Flagstaff, Arizona, went to the doctor after bouts of coughing that she'd had for months and that would not go away. She remembers fearing she had pneumonia. But after comprehensive medical tests, she would learn she had Thymoma carcinoma, a rare type of thymus gland cancer that is slow growing, carries a low risk of recurrence, and has a good survival rate. She was advised to go to University Medical Center (UMC) in Tucson because they had a team of medical experts who specialized in treating this rare type of cancer.

On the drive from Flagstaff to Tucson for the appointment, the symptoms worsened, and the mother of four was raced to the ER when she found herself struggling to breathe. Gloria remembers hearing the Code Blue blast over the hospital speaker and the unified cry of the medical team: "We're losing her." Miraculously, after surgery and an extended stay at UMC, Gloria hung on and fought through. The specialists told her they had removed a tumor embedded in her lung that was the size of a football.

Over the course of the next nine years, Gloria successfully battled cancer twice. The first was in 2002, just two years after she'd been given a clean bill of health from her first bout in 1995; the second occurrence was in late 2004. She underwent surgeries, chemo, and radiation treatments. In the process, she lost her left lung and left rib cage. Each time, she put up a valiant fight and eventually was back in the classroom doing what inspired her the most, teaching young children.

Things had been back to normal for about five years when, in the summer of 2010, Gloria started getting severe abdominal pain, could not hold down any food, and was having severe sweats followed by severe chills. Naturally, her fear was that the cancer had returned. After over two months of fighting this condition while taking a battery of tests, it was determined that she was having gallbladder attacks and needed emergency *surgery. Once again, with family and friends by her side, she fully recovered from this ordeal; soon afterward she was back in the classroom.*

Gloria's good health was short-lived. Toward the end of 2010, she found herself short of breath while performing the simplest tasks. She continued teaching but was finding it very challenging to work through the full day. She went for a medical checkup and was told that her heart's ejection rate was functioning at 27 percent. Because she had only one lung, the doctors recommended that she get a defibrillator to aid her breathing. The procedure was scheduled for early February 2011; however, the weekend before the appointment, Gloria was back in the hospital, this time with pneumonia. As always, she remained positive and prayerful and maintained a very inspiring attitude. She firmly believed that, with God's blessings, she would overcome this obstacle and be able to get the much-needed defibrillator. Gloria was in the hospital for a few days and eventually fully recovered at home. She was thankful to have overcome the pneumonia and returned to her classroom once again.

Because the doctors wanted Gloria to be physically strong, her appointment for the defibrillator was delayed a couple of months, until April 4, 2011. However, on the morning of April 1, her 55th birthday, she suffered a massive stroke.

Although Gloria has made a remarkable recovery

from her bouts with cancer and the stroke, this enthu-
siastic and dedicated grade school teacher, former travel
women's league tennis player, and mother of four has
faced a significant change of pace and important changes
in life. All these events, from 1995 through 2011, had
a cumulative impact on Gloria's overall health. She has
only one lung, has limited mobility of her right arm, has
constant cramps in her right foot, and has only peripheral
vision in her left eye; her memory is foggy at times, and
her energy level is not what it was. In spite of all this, she
remains strong-willed, has an inspiring spirit, and is quick
to state that she has been blessed.

"I've been so lucky and blessed to have so many
good people carry me and my family through this," says
Gloria.

Those words, "I am so blessed," have become the mantra
and first words Gloria Linn says when asked to share
her almost 20-year journey, which started when she was
diagnosed with this rare cancer. They are the four words
that she says have kept her from completely sinking. The
encouraging news is that doctors are getting better at
catching cancer at an early stage and helping people like
Gloria live—albeit between reoccurring bouts—as cancer
survivors.

Many, like Gloria, have come to rely on friends and
loved ones for help. Immediately following the first

diagnosis of cancer, her mother, husband Jesús, and six siblings stepped in to help out. She is very touched by the level of support she received from her friends, who also cooked meals, sat at her side during chemotherapy, and cared for her children, ages 8 to 16 (in 1995)—driving them to school and extracurricular activities, taking them to movies and fun activities, and holding prayer circles for Gloria. Throughout the last nearly 20 years, and to this day, Gloria's support system has remained strong.

Here, she shares some of the pivotal moments that she is especially grateful for:

THE WRITE STUFF

When her insurance company refused to approve costs for an expensive PET scan procedure, parents, students, and fellow teachers at the elementary school where Gloria had been a teacher sent more than 400 handwritten letters and made dozens of phone calls on Gloria's behalf to the president of the insurance company. It took four months, but finally the procedure was approved. "They saved my life," she says.

POINTS OF LIGHT

When Gloria's cancer returned for the third time in 2004, two significant events happened that Gloria says she will eternally be thankful for. One: the crowd of friends who showed up on her doorstep with points of light and singing prayers; two: students at the elementary school she taught at dedicated their eighth-grade graduation to her.

Gloria continued to teach throughout most of her ill health. One day, her co-workers asked her, "What can we do? How can we help?" Gloria replied, "Your prayers are much appreciated—maybe go to church and light a novena candle." Then, looking at one teacher whom she knew was not a churchgoer, she smiled and jokingly said, "And from you, my dear friend, a sparkler will do!" It didn't take much time before the group made plans, unbeknownst to Gloria, to walk up her cul-de-sac one evening, singing prayers of hope as they held sparklers. She recalls thinking the knock at her door was someone delivering a meal, an event which had become commonplace. To her great surprise, it was a group of 70 to 80 friends and neighbors who had gathered in song and prayer on her behalf. It's a moment that she's thankful for, and she cherishes it to this day.

BIRDS OF FLIGHT

Gloria was invited to their school's eighth-grade graduation ceremony. When she settled into her seat and was reviewing the program's booklet before the ceremony started, she noticed her name was listed as "Guest of Honor." Gloria's former students (the eighth-grade graduates) had been deeply moved reading about Sadako Sasaki, a two-year-old Japanese girl who was at home in 1945 when the first Hiroshima bomb exploded. At age 11, Sadako was diagnosed with leukemia, hospitalized, and given almost a year to live. Her friend came to the hospital and folded a piece of gold paper into the shape of a paper crane, a reference to the ancient Japanese story promising that anyone who folds a thousand origami cranes will be granted a wish by the gods. A popular version of the story is that Sadako fell short of her goal of folding 1,000 cranes, having folded only 644 before her death, and that her friends completed the 1,000 and buried them all with her. The story is chronicled in the book *Sadako and the Thousand Paper Cranes*. "I was told the students said, 'If they did it for a little girl in Japan, why can't we do it for Mrs. Linn?'" she says. And so the students folded up 1,000 paper cranes with various "get well" messages; they presented a golden crane to her that evening and told her 1,000 paper cranes were being delivered to her classroom. She says, "It was one of the most memorable events of my life."

HER ANGEL, HER HUSBAND

Through it all, Gloria's husband, Jesús Linn, has stood firmly at her side, and has worked hard as a civil engineering technologist to help the family stay financially afloat. He spent many overnights at the hospital, staying by Gloria's bedside. He constantly maintained complete composure and always made certain Gloria had whatever she needed to be nurtured back to good health. He has been, as she puts it, "truly, my angel."

HER FAMILY

Gloria grew up in Douglas, Arizona, in a family of seven children. Her parents brought the family from Mexico to Douglas, with a vision that their children would all graduate from high school and college. Most of her siblings did exactly that; five completed advanced degrees. "My parents gave us a strong spiritual foundation and instilled in us that, even in the midst of the hardest times, we would always find blessings," she says. She often wonders about the health risks that came from living in Douglas, especially since an older brother was diagnosed with a cancerous brain tumor and died at age four; a younger sister was stillborn; her dear sister Delia was diagnosed with a rare form of ovarian cancer and died in February 2004, one day shy of her 49th birthday; and another sister has battled lupus for over 30 years.

PENNIES FROM HEAVEN

Gloria and her sisters have always considered pennies found on the ground to be "pennies from heaven," pennies that their mom and dad send to them. When her sister Delia was in the hospital, Gloria and another sister sat by Delia's side through the night. Although Delia had been in a coma, the medical staff said Delia could still hear and encouraged them to talk to her. At one point Gloria remembers saying, "Delia, you know how mom and dad send us pennies from heaven? Send us nickels! Then we'll know these are from you!" Following Gloria's third battle with cancer, her sister, two brothers, a sister-in-law, a nephew, cousins, and friends made a 50-mile walking pilgrimage from Nogales, Arizona, to Magdalena, Sonora. It was a two-day trip during what were some of the hottest days of the season. Along the way, when Gloria would feel too weak to keep walking and carry on, she found a nickel on the ground, while at the same time her sister found a penny. This find put a spring back in their step. Gloria says that, to this day, finding nickels and pennies always warms her heart and puts a smile on her face.

"No matter what new hurdle gets thrown in my path, I have had angels at my side all the way," says Gloria. "I've been covered in the blessings of others, and I have no doubt that that is why I have gotten through all of this."

GRATEFUL LIFE PRACTICE

"I think of my friends and family who have constantly been by my side and give thanks daily, often throughout the day. And I say my prayers each night before I go to bed."

GRATITUDE AS MEDICINE

Thankfulness can fire you up, cool you down, and help you push away depression, according to Martin Seligman, Ph.D., a pioneer in the positive psychology movement, and his colleagues at the University of Pennsylvania.

Gratitude is a powerful antidote to depression, the researchers found after delivering instructions to 50 severely depressed visitors to a self-help website. They recommended that individuals take time each day to write down three things that went well that day, and why they thought so.

Fifteen days later, almost 95 percent of the people said they felt significantly less depressed. Their scores on a widely used depression inventory dropped by 50 percent—equivalent to improvement seen with medication or psychotherapy. Individuals in a placebo-controlled group who wrote down three childhood memories each day did not experience an improvement in their depressive symptoms.

More important, the effects for the group practicing gratitude lasted for a full six months. The researchers repeated the same study several months later with a different group of depressed web users and obtained substantially the same results. Seligman's group also found that writing in a gratitude journal had a mood-boosting effect for depressed patients in a 12-week therapy group, as well as for patients in individual therapy.

In a separate study included in the Journal of Personality and Social Psychology, 84 percent of Americans said expressing gratitude reduces stress and depression and fosters better health and optimism. You can read more here: psycnet.apa.org/journals/psp/84/2/377.

CHAPTER SEVEN

THE LINK BETWEEN SPIRITUALITY AND GRATITUDE: CREATING UNEXPECTED GRACE AND PEACE

The movement of grace in our lives toward freedom is a mystery. So we simply say "Thanks." Something had to open, something had to give, and I don't have a clue how to get things to do that. But they did, or grace did. Thank you. An invisible shift happens through the broken places.

—Anne Lamott

Many of the world's religions include the call to grace as a central tenet of their teachings. Giving thanks to God and other deities is a universal theme in Christian, Buddhist, Muslim, Jewish, and Hindu traditions. Gratitude is the keystone of so many ceremonial rituals; in the Orthodox, Catholic and Anglican Churches, the name for the most important rite, the Eucharist, is derived from a Greek word—*eucharistia*—which translates as *thanksgiving*. It's no wonder that religious people are apt to have a greater sense of gratitude in life.

It has been only recently that scientists have linked

this practice of gratitude to a corresponding increase in happiness. The latest data compiled by researchers at Pew Research Center, a nonpartisan fact tank, found that adults who attended religious services once a week or more were significantly more likely to report feeling "very happy" (36 percent) than those who attended seldom or never (23 percent), and less likely to say they were "pretty happy" (46 percent vs. 55 percent) or "not too happy" (13 percent vs. 19 percent). Those who attend services more than once a week are the happiest of all, with 43 percent reporting that they are "very happy." This correlation between happiness and spirituality has been corroborated by numerous scientific studies.

Experiments conducted by Jo-Ann Tsang, an associate professor of psychology at Baylor University, found that just thinking about religion can cause people to feel and act more gratefully. For those who don't belong to a religion, but commit to a practice of gratitude on a consistent basis, the results can be the same. Worship gives people a place to give thanks, and offers prayers to contemplate or chant. Many of these prayers and lessons are underscored with messages of gratitude. However, giving thanks for blessings—whether or not one is affiliated with an organized religion—can be a form of spirituality, and many people report that it gives them the same benefits.

ADOPTING GRATITUDE: PORTRAIT OF HOPE AND A LITTLE GUY NAMED XIA

However motherhood comes to you, it's a miracle.
　　　　　　　　　　—Valerie Harper, adoptive parent

The picture on Tricia Treft's Facebook status says it all. It's a passport-sized photo of a precious four-year-old boy in a green and beige anime cartoon "Lucky Boy" T-shirt. His name is Xia, pronounced Chee-aw.

The comments following Tricia's posting, "Bring Xia to Chicago," speak volumes: "Welcome, little man!" "He is adorable." "What a sweetheart." "So happy for you." "Such a beautiful child…. What a journey of new adventures, love, and blessings is in store for all of you!!!" "Oh Tricia, what a precious little face & smile. Praying God will fill your home with love, fun, security, & adventure! Love & hugs coming your way."

Already, this little guy has stretched the hearts and spirits of her and her husband, Garry's, love in many ways, says Tricia. The couple will host Xia for four weeks starting in mid-December 2013, when Xia will travel halfway around the world to their Westmont, Illinois home. The opportunity is being made possible through a unique program, called Project 143 (www.projectonefortythree.org), that arranges for older Chinese orphan children to spend an unforgettable month with host families in the United States. The ultimate goal is for the couple to be able to adopt Xia. But that is another minimum six-month journey to apply for formal adoption after Xia returns to China.

For now, Tricia says every fiber of her being is focused on giving thanks for the child who is coming, albeit for a limited time, to share the Christmas holiday. As a hospital chaplain and spiritual director, Tricia knows there are always two ways to look at something: through the negative lens of stress, sadness, fear, and difficulty, or by holding this opportunity in the light of her strong faith and viewing it as a grace-filled passage to grow and be creative in devising a solution for her longing to be a mom. Here, Tricia shares the more than two-decade journey she and Garry embarked on to build a family.

As a child, Tricia experienced many extended stays at hospitals for treatment of hypoglycemia and asthma. She knew early on that her life purpose would be to help others facing medical crises. "Because of my own illnesses, I always felt comfortable in hospitals and wanted to find an opportunity to bring grace and faith to others who were ill," she says. "I guess I realized I had an ability to understand a tiny glimpse of what they were going through."

Fast-forward to today. The 44-year-old is the Pastoral Care Manager for Adventist Hinsdale Hospital in the western suburbs of Chicago. There, she leads a team of five chaplains in providing spiritual care to patients, families, and staff, and oversees a spiritual ambassador's voluntary program that fosters spiritual nurturing for nurses, doctors, and other healthcare providers and staff. In addition, she is a spiritual director at Mayslake Ministries (www.MayslakeMinistries.org), a lay-led Christian organization in Lombard, Illinois, where she provides spiritual direction for women struggling with infertility issues, miscarriages, and the loss of children. She also helped launch a "Walk to Remember Garden," for families who have lost a baby through miscarriage or stillbirth, on the second-floor patio of the hospital. The garden provides a special healing place to remember the babies.

Since 2008, she has been on call almost 24/7 to provide comfort and care for patients and families in the throes of a Code Blue crisis, through hospice end-of-life journeys, and in the Neonatal Intensive Care Unit following a miscarriage or the illness or loss of a child.

Though childhood illness drove her commitment to help people through the hard times of medical illness, she had no idea that the challenges facing patients at the hospital would become her own.

In fact, life seemed to be on a beautiful track as she pursued her education in spiritual direction and pastoral care, graduating in 2011 with a D.Min. from McCormick Theological Seminary, following 20-plus years of college and master's studies. In seminary, she also met Garry, and the couple celebrated their 21st wedding anniversary on March 21, 2014.

Garry is the Administrative Coordinator in the Department of Behavioral Medicine Programs at Midwestern University. From the get-go, he and Tricia were a family, and at the same time were making a difference in other people's lives through their work. But they thought about the question, "What makes a family?" all the time. And they wanted to create one of their own.

About 10 years after Tricia and Garry were married, they felt ready to begin a family. Unfortunately, their journey to parenthood came with an unexpected struggle, a litany of infertility issues. During those years of trying to conceive again and again in hopes of finally carrying a child to term, Tricia went through the wringer to become a mother. During those years, her sister's family grew to 10 children. Tricia says she feels blessed that God brought this extended family of children—nieces and nephews—into their lives.

Through it all, they kept hoping and praying for children. "Sometimes it has been very sad, but God has always been there to help us get through and has been very faithful with blessings for both of us," she says. "God blessed us with lots of nieces and nephews and friends with children who generously included us in their families," she says. "But we still held a longing to try to figure out how we could make an even greater impact in a child's life."

In 2007, they began the adoption process and have been waiting for a traditional Chinese adoption for the last six years.

Tricia and Garry soon discovered the intensity with which they care deeply about orphans around the world. So when the opportunity to host a Chinese orphan for four weeks at Christmas came up through the Chinese adoption agency they have been working with, they said yes. Project143.org (named for the 143 million orphans around the globe) provides the opportunity for an orphan to become part of a family, experiencing the power of belonging, connectedness, love, and family. Host children range in age from six to 16, and each host family is allowed to choose the child that fits best with their family dynamic after viewing the children's photos and reading their biographies online. Without hosting, most of these children will eventually "age out" of the system and never experience the life-giving, life-changing love that family provides. Hosting can also serve as a connection between an orphan and his or her "forever family."

Though the timeline for Xia's visit is limited, as all children must return to China after the four weeks, many children, including Xia, are also adoption eligible. "This is our wish: to possibly bring Xia home to live next year," Tricia says. "This opportunity with Project 143 helps us impact a child's life forever. We've been asked if we have the option to consider adoption, and the answer is yes. We are taking it one step at a time, and will see if this is where God is leading our family to join together through adoption in the future.

"We intend to share our family, our friends, our church, and the fun things of Chicago with our little friend. Most importantly, we hope to share our love for God with him," says Tricia. "We share our story for you to share in our joy and thank you for sharing in prayer and cheer."

However Xia's connection to their family turns out, Garry and Tricia treasured the four weeks when they welcomed the six-year-old into their home during December 2013 and rung in the new year of 2014.

But before Xia arrived, during the period we wrote this story, Tricia and Garry focused on the logistics. The most common question Tricia and Garry have heard so far is, "What language will you speak to Xia?" Her answer: "While we don't know for sure, we'll learn a little Chinese, hopefully he'll learn a lot of English, and we'll speak smiles and love." The second question is, "What will he eat?" From some communiqués, they know Xia likes noodles and candy. "So far, so good," she says. The comfort and solace Xia will bring to their lives, and the love they hope to bring to his "will be the greatest reward in life," says Tricia. "So many people are wishing us well and we are so grateful for the joy we get to experience as we share our love in his life." And she's thinking, "We'll have to introduce him to tacos."

GRATEFUL LIFE PRACTICE

Giving back is Tricia's way of practicing gratitude in daily life. She suggests finding ways to help others who are experiencing the same challenges you have gone through or are going through now. To that end, she volunteers as a spiritual director at MayslakeMinistries.org, providing direction and comfort to other women and men facing the challenge of infertility. She also helped create a garden to honor families who have experienced miscarriages and stillborn births. Gratitude is helping others who are suffering feel nourished and alive again.

THE POWER OF PRAYER

To Muslims, prayer is a ladder, a journey reaching to heaven. St. Therese of Lisieux called it "an uplifting of the heart." In the words of William James, "prayer is the soul and essence of religion," and to Auguste Sabatier, it is "religion in action." According to the Dakota Sioux physician and author Ohiyesa, "In the life of the Indian there was only one inevitable duty—the duty of prayer—the daily recognition of the Unseen and Eternal." Mahatma Gandhi practiced a "prayer that needs no speech," and Thomas Merton struggled for a form of prayer in everyday life "with everything I touch." For Brother David Steindl-Rast, "Prayer is unlimited mindfulness."

—Phil Cousineau

BODY AND POLE:
DANCING HER WAY TO EMPOWERMENT

We ask ourselves, who am I to be brilliant, gorgeous, handsome, talented, and fabulous? Actually, who are you not to be?

—Nelson Mandela

In April 2012, Erin L'Hotta thought she was happily married and was poised to jump to the next level of her career with the promise of an exciting new position as a social media strategist for a Fortune 500 company just on the horizon. Two months later, her husband of four years bolted, leaving her for another woman. By October, she was 28 and divorced.

"*There really was no conversation. He made a decision to end our marriage, and there was nothing I could do or say that would change his mind,*" *she says.* "*Basically, he just abandoned me.*"

Erin's friends immediately stepped in to form a circle of support. One friend urged her to do something to nurture herself. Her suggestion: pole dancing. She offered to be Erin's workout partner.

Erin deliberated for a half a second and said: "Why not?" As a child she had loved dancing and had been a skilled gymnast through high school. Even though she knew some might snicker—pole dancing has been and continues to be associated with strippers and the exploitation of women—Erin saw beyond the stereotyping. She liked the idea of a good workout and tapping into her love of dancing. She packed a pair of high heels into her work bag and basically told the world: Watch out, here I come.

"I always loved to dance, but never danced during my marriage," says Erin. "I wouldn't wish getting divorced on anyone. But somehow I realized that it opened up the freedom for me to do anything. It was a reset button."

Today, Erin is dancing her way around the pole, pursuing this universal and beautiful form of self-expression. But it's not just about the exercise and the new freedom of expression; it's become a metaphor for the spiritual journey she has embarked on in recent years. The words she uses to describe herself on Pinterest encourage us all to search for something more in our lives and to appreciate the gifts that make us unique: Writer. Dancer. Orchid-grower. Lover of poetry, mountains, and Miyabe maple trees.

When you want to grow, the hardest thing is shedding who you used to be and to set new goals in a new direction. Most would like to tiptoe into that transition, but, as Erin discovered, divorce has a funny way of yanking the Band-Aid off. What led to her husband's seemingly sudden departure is nuanced and complex.

Two years earlier, Erin found herself beset by debilitating anxiety attacks. "Essentially, I was afraid of everything," she recalls. In hindsight, she says she always felt as if there was "a heaviness, like a ball and chain, during my marriage that wouldn't go away, no matter how much I tried to find healthy ways to manage my anxiety."

When her husband left, so did the heaviness. But Erin found herself yearning for more, eager to forge a new life and a new path for herself.

She discovered that when trying to make a change for the better, sometimes it's easier to focus on what you don't have or on everything that's going wrong.

For a short while, she found herself doing exactly that.

But, by bringing gratitude into her focus, she found healing and forgiveness, as well as a sense of mindfulness and appreciation in the present. Gratitude, she discovered, opens the heart and connects us to our self, to others, and to the world through our appreciation for what is.

What's unique is the way Erin found to ritualize gratitude: pole dancing.

At first she practiced a tentative strut around the pole, wrapping herself around it in intriguing ways, but quickly found that it reconnected her to the flow and "welcomed release" she used to feel as a child dancing. It also turned into an amazing, empowering workout.

"Think ballet barre turned vertical," Erin explains. "It's a combination of rock climbing, ballet, and yoga. It makes you feel strong within yourself. It unleashes your physical power, and your body transforms in the process. I mean, how many people can say that they can hang 180 degrees sideways on a pole from one knee? If that doesn't empower you, I don't know what does."

In addition to exercise, the pole became a spiritual tool to assist Erin in letting go of the things that no longer served her in exchange for the new ideas and habits that were transforming her and giving birth to a whole new healthy lifestyle. Her soul began to feel infused with new life and a sense that, as Julian of Norwich describes it, "All will be well."

For Erin, pole dancing has opened up a whole new outlet of expression. "It's allowed a new part of me to come alive," she adds. "In many ways I am grateful my husband left me, because I have tapped into a whole new part of me and made some amazing new friendships."

On some days Erin says she feels like Peter Pan or a ballerina, finding joy in her life again. She's also connected to a sisterhood of friends, many who also took to the pole to mend and reinvent after relationship breakups.

"It's crazy, I never would have met all these friends if he hadn't left, and it feels like we were always supposed to be friends," she says. "The gift he has given me is that I am a totally different person. I am a dancer who embraces adventure and new challenges, and is living a life that's joy-filled and anxiety-free again. I am grateful for that amazing transformation that would not have happened otherwise."

And last summer, after honoring her new life as a single woman and staying in most weekends because she just didn't feel like getting into the dating scene—or going out, for that matter—Erin accepted a co-worker's invitation to attend a party.

At the Fourth of July BBQ, she met "the new love of my life." He asked her if she wanted to dance, and now, months later, their relationship and Erin's spirit are soaring.

"I feel so alive and free," she says. "And now I have my man dancing beside me."

GRATEFUL LIFE PRACTICE

Unlike the negative stereotypes pole dancing has received in the media, there is no stripping involved. Twice a week, Erin dons yoga / gymnastics-type workout attire and for the length of the class (90 minutes), she meditates and stretches, followed by different repetitions of pull-ups on the pole to warm up. Then her pole dance teacher focuses

Erin on practicing two or three specific pole tricks in a given class, followed by a dance routine combining everything she's learned.

IN HER ELEMENT: FINDING RENEWAL FROM CHRONIC ILLNESS BY IMMERSING HERSELF IN GRATITUDE

Walk boldly through your life with an open, broken heart.

—Joanna Macy

Carla Valentino is lying on a padded table, clutching the side bars, as electrodes are applied up and down her body, sending chilling electrical pulses. She is undergoing a Calmare treatment, a technologically advanced solution that has been highly effective in the treatment of chemotherapy-induced peripheral neuropathy.

The 45-year-old mother of two from Land O'Lakes, Florida, has travelled to Boynton Beach, Florida, to seek relief for a progressive chronic nerve disorder that has robbed most of her mobility and left her dependent on others. The treatment involves staying in a hotel five days *a week for three weeks and costs $1,000 a week, just for the procedure. Prior to the onset of illness, Carla was an active fashion boutique owner when she slipped and broke her ankle, triggering the last six years of chronic and debilitating illness.*

The illness has forced her to surrender her "mom" duties like carpooling her children, Brett, 13, and Natalie, eight, to school and their activities, along with running her business. On the worst days, it keeps her bedridden— on the best, writhing in pain but able to maneuver with crutches, a cane, or a wheelchair.

In November 2013 she is on her 10th Calmare treatment, and a couple of times she's felt her excruciating pain level drop. But during this, her last treatment, tears are flowing and she has to be carried out of the medical facility. The experimental treatment did not work. "It was a major disappointment," she says.

Carla has learned not to try to suppress the waves of her pain. Instead she rides through them, lets the tears erupt, and stays in the mystery, as her way to liberate herself from the clutch of the illness.

Despite the roller-coaster of emotions that comes with facing chronic illness and a series of failed treatments and remedies, one of the most potent and nurturing antidotes has been intentionally focusing on the blessings, says Carla.

"I have found and find strength through my faith, a

positive attitude, and being grateful for my family's love and support," she says. "I push through being depressed about another failure. And at the same time, I am still grateful something new came along. It's encouraging to know that research is continuing."

As she stumbles through the healthcare maze seeking relief from her pain, Carla looks with hope to a potential cure or remedy on the horizon. She knows that survival means evolving. She has set her intention for living: to live with a grateful heart.

Six years ago, Carla Valentino was at a birthday party with her two young children, joining in the fun and jumping around the bounce house. She slipped and severely sprained her ankle. Several months later she was diagnosed with Reflex Sympathetic Dystrophy Syndrome, also known as RSDS, a progressive illness of the autonomic nervous system. It's a multi-symptom condition affecting one, two, or sometimes all four of the extremities.

"The worst reality was when my kids asked why I couldn't play with them as actively as I used to," she says.

Her husband, David, who was then her fiancé, immediately jumped into the role of round-the-clock caregiver, cooking, taking care of the children, and driving her to doctor and PT appointments. Her 82-year-old mom also comes to Florida periodically to help with the kids when Carla has had a surgical or outpatient treatment, and one of her best friends helps carpool her kids to and from school and their after-school activities.

Over the past six years, Carla has had 24 injections in her spine (including Ketamine and snail poison). In between doctors' appointments and physical therapy, she keeps close observation on the pain and her condition. She also undergoes many forms of therapy, including structural energetic therapy, cranial and laser therapies, chiropractic treatments, hypnosis, and yoga. Meditation, visualization, and breathing exercises are part of her daily tool kit too. "It's challenging taking medication because it affects my system and clouds my mind," she says.

"The hardest part is trying to balance being a wife and mother when I have to depend on others to do much of this for me," she says. "Daily I wake up and don't know the level of pain and/or spasms that I will have to deal with. There are mornings when my pain is what I call my 'do-able' pain, when I can put some pressure on my foot but cannot walk for a long period of time. And then there are the really bad days when it takes over."

In an effort to explain her condition to her daughter, Carla embarked on a journey to write a book specifically for children, on how to understand and cope with illness. *When Can We Run, Dance, and Play Again?* (Author House), is a colorful, touching and informative children's story for children of parents who are suffering from chronic pain and illness.

"When you toss in a medical condition that feels as if it's constantly attacking itself, and you have kids with busy schedules and a husband, it's challenging," she says. "I never know from one minute to the next my pain level and if my foot will have a spasm. Of course there is the daily medication which affects your mind, soul, and spirit. It is imperative to find whatever it takes to find a balance. If not, the world will collapse around you and you will be in a dark hole."

So began her decision to treat herself with a daily infusion of gratitude.

"Every day I wake up grateful for what I have," she says. "My family, friends, animals, being alive, support, love, and the fact that my life could be worse. I make sure I smile. I say thank you to people who help me."

She adds, "Many times, when I give thanks, I speak in my head or out loud and I visualize a happy, positive place. Somewhere I feel at peace, tranquil. It helps me to release any negative energy so I can allow positive energy in. I could be in the shower or outside enjoying the day. It doesn't matter as long as I am taking a few moments for myself."

Last fall, Carla also tried another new treatment—a Ketamine compound to put on her foot every night for two weeks.

"After I put the compound on, I wrapped it with Saran Wrap and left it on for 20 minutes. I hate to sound like a broken record, but unfortunately it did nothing but irritate my foot. My pain level went through the roof! I never took off the wrap. I bore the tremendous pain hoping that, by getting through it, my RSDS would improve. The hardest part is to see the sadness in my husband and kids' eyes. I feel the need to lift their spirits and tell them it's okay. This means that there is something else out there for me. Until then, I can't beat myself up about it.

"The biggest part of my life that has been affected has been my family. My family means the world to me, and, when I see them suffer watching me suffer, it kills me. My mom is 82, and to watch her cry and break down while she is watching me in pain, breaks my heart. My kids miss their 'old' mom, a mom who could spontaneously pick up and go, a mom who doesn't have to spend days in bed. My kids have watched me in extreme pain, and it makes me feel guilty.

"Years ago I was able to run around. I would go and then go some more. But I can be creative! We have painted and played cards and board games while I have to stay in bed. It does help with the guilt a little, and we stay connected as a family.

"My husband and I met one year before my injury. David misses how independent I was and how we would go dancing, make plans that we could commit to, and have me whole, without constant pain."

Growing up, Carla says, she was a combination of

tomboy and girly girl and was very active. "I loved to skateboard, ride dirt bikes, and collect rocks, but I also loved dressing up. Prior to my injury, I went through a change in life, through divorce, and I started a T-shirt and clothing line—BonChic Designs. But due to my injury and treatments, I had to close my business."

She says, "Many of my friends have stuck by me, but many have also left my side. They do not understand what I go through, no matter how much I explain to them about RSDS. I think some are afraid. They do not know how to handle what I have."

No matter what she does, Carla says, her RSDS seems to want to take her over. But, she adds, "I won't allow it. I will continue to pray, be thankful, visualize, center myself, and believe in my thoughts and what I put out there. Keeping positive people around me, music, and other things that make me happy helps keep me sane."

In December 2013, her "gratitude treatments" manifested themselves, she says. Having formerly owned and operated her own fashion business, she had to give it up when the illness became too much. It broke her heart.

"I believe that one of my 'thoughts' was answered," she says. "I stumbled across a boutique I fell in love with, called Basic Black Collection. I brought in several people, helped them put a wardrobe together. The owner, Sydney, e-mailed me and asked if we could meet. We did, and Sydney offered me a personal shopper position! She knows I have RSDS, and she said, 'Just do what you have been doing, and I'll pay you.' Since then I have brought in several people, and we also had an evening party where I invited several people, and it was a hit! It was a very successful night."

"For this to happen to me, for Sydney to know I have a chronic illness and offer me a position, I am extremely grateful!

"You never know," she goes on, "what life is going to throw at you. You can either lock yourself in a room and wither away or be positive and grateful. I choose being positive and grateful. It may not take my pain away, but it makes life a lot easier."

GRATEFUL LIFE PRACTICE: TIPS FOR FINDING THE GRATITUDE IN EVERY DAY

Take time for prayer. Every morning after waking up, Carla says, before she does anything else, "I close my eyes and give thanks to God and to the universe for giving me strength to cope with the challenges that lie ahead. I also give thanks in this prayer for what is positive in my life."

Focus on the good things. Make a point to give thanks for the good things in your life, even in the midst of pain and chaos. For Carla that means saying thanks every day for her children, family, and parents, family pets, and the fact that she is alive and can feel love.

Visualize what gives you joy. In times of adversity,

Carla says it is important to visualize and be grateful for the places where you have been happy and positive in your life. They will help counteract the negative energy you feel when you are feeling challenged and help create the peace you are looking for.

NAIKAN: THE JAPANESE PHILOSOPHY
ROOTED IN GRATITUDE

Naikan is a Japanese word that means *inside looking* or *introspection*. It is a method of self-reflection developed by Yoshimoto Ishin, a businessman and devout Jodo Shinshu Buddhist, in the 1940s. Although it has its roots in Buddhism, Naikan has no religious context. In *The End of Your Life Book Club* by Will Schwalbe, he recalls the teachings of Naikan, which remind people to be grateful for everything. "If you are sitting in a chair, you need to realize that someone made that chair, and someone sold it, and someone delivered it—and you are the beneficiary of all that. Just because they didn't do it especially for you doesn't mean you aren't blessed to be using it and enjoying it. The idea is that, if you practice Naikan, life becomes a series of small miracles, and you may start to notice everything that goes right in a typical life and not the few things that go wrong."

Today, there are about 40 Naikan centers in Japan, and Naikan is used in mental health counseling, addiction treatment, rehabilitation of prisoners, schools, and business.

Naikan is based on three basic questions:

What have I received?

What have I given?

What troubles and difficulties have I caused?

A CIRCLE OF FRIENDS: SOUL FRIENDS CREATE
AN ANCIENT CIRCLE OF BELONGING

A FRIENDSHIP BLESSING

May you be blessed with good friends.

May you learn to be a good friend to yourself.

May you be able to journey to that place in your soul
    where

there is great love, warmth, feeling, and forgiveness.
    May this change you.

May it transfigure that which is negative, distant, or
    cold in you.

May you be brought into the real passion, kinship,
    and affinity of belonging.

May you treasure your friends.

    May you be good to them and may you be there
    for them;

may they bring you all the blessing, challenges, truth,
and light that you need for your journey.

May you never be isolated.

May you always be in the gentle nest of belonging
    with your *anam ċara.*

—*John O'Donohue*

MARY BETH'S STORY

In the Celtic tradition, friends are thought to be united by soul-love; the old Gaelic term for this is "anam ċara." Anam is the word for soul, and ċara is the word for friend. The concept makes for a lovely book, Anam Cara: A Book of Celtic Wisdom, *by John O'Donohue. I love this book. I've read it many times, and it's a favorite gift for friends and family. To me it is a guide for living a thoughtful and deep life, recognizing our own belonging and the belonging of others in the universe. It taught me to look for the sacred in others.*

According to the book, when you are with your anam ċaras, you are free to share your innermost self, your mind and your heart. "This friendship is an act of recognition and belonging," O'Donohue writes. "You are joined in an ancient and eternal way with the 'friend of your soul.'"

The Celtic understanding is that there are no limitations of space or time with the soul. The bond is indissoluble. In the practice of yoga, it's kind of the same thing. Friends greet friends with Namaskar *("I salute the God in You").*

This leads to my story about a circle of friends who are connected like an umbilical cord to the birthplace of our ancestors.

Three years ago, my youngest daughter, Emily, was poised to head off to college. My father had recently passed, and I was caring for my aging mother, who was very sad, and, unbeknownst to me, was entering a journey of deteriorating health that required a lot of visits to doctors' offices and birthed in me an urgency to help her pain go away.

I spent the summer with Emily, shopping the aisles of Bed, Bath & Beyond; scouring the Internet for futons; and trying to hide my tears that "my baby" would be flying from the nest (and was buzzing with excitement over the color of her towels and the dorm decorating plans with her roommate). At the same time, during the late nights in the ER, and the Sunday afternoon lunches and treks to bring light into my mom's life, I also could see what awaited on the road ahead.

I made a point to start preparing myself for both letting-go's.

We rescued a second dog; I signed up for yoga classes; way overbooked my work life; made plans to meet every friend and colleague I've ever known in my life come college drop-off; and signed up for volunteer projects as if I were the Bill and Melinda Gates of the Northwest. I became almost obsessed about trying to fill the anticipated void that I feared I'd be facing when I was home alone with four bedrooms to choose from every night.

The real treat I gave myself was saying "yes" to the invitation from Paddy, the owner of the cute little Irish store, "Paddy's on the Square," in the neighboring town of Long Grove, to join a book club the store was launching. I had stumbled into the store to buy a copy of *Anam Cara* for a close friend who had just lost her husband. He asked me if I liked to read, and of course my face lit up. "Read? I love to read," I remember responding. "I'm a writer." Not sure why I told him the writer part.

In some ways, I wanted to stay connected to my family's Irish roots and figured this would be an easy way to do that.

I signed up.

I still remember the night of my first meeting. It was snowing softly, and Christmas carols were filling the cobblestone square the shop is named for. I headed upstairs to the attic of Paddy's, which is built to look like a cottage home in Ireland. Tea and scones were served, and I immersed myself in this community of mostly women who were passionate about the characters and storylines of books. Both my parents were avid readers and, as a child, I discovered a whole new world the moment I could read my first book. After the evening, the members headed over to the village pub.

The books we read were books I probably would never have picked up on the shelves of Barnes & Noble. They were penned by Irish authors telling the stories of the Irish, and they took me on a journey to my family's homeland.

But the real blessing came in my friendships with the circle of friends in the club. A recognition opened as we deciphered the stories and shared the inner secrets of the tales and our shared connectedness to these Irish characters. And that is where the mystery and the divine comes in.

As we shared our own stories, it would turn out that not one, not two, but five of us—KC, Cathy, Marion, Maureen, and me—have grandparents born in County Mayo, and not just in the county, in the same small town, Ballina, a community of less than 10,000 people in north County Mayo that lies at the mouth of the River Moy near Killala Bay.

It is overwhelming to think that my grandma, Bridget Crowley McMahon, lived in the same town as their grandmas, and most likely were friends. Over the course of the three years, I was able to unite my Uncle Tommy with KC's uncle TP, who were boyhood friends together in Ballina. And I have come to learn that there truly is an eternal embrace of friendship that runs through our lives and connects us all and, as O'Donohue says, "gives us permission to enter this ancient circle of belonging."

There is a beautiful Trinitarian motif running through Celtic spirituality. This little invocation captures this:

The Sacred Three
My fortress be
encircling me
Come and be round
my hearth and my home.

CHAPTER EIGHT

HOW GRATITUDE HELPS YOU DISCOVER YOUR DESIRES AND ACHIEVE YOUR DREAMS

Three keys to more abundant living: caring about others, daring for others, sharing with others.

—William A. Ward

How exactly does the practice of gratitude attract abundance? The key is that abundance is already there. Once you notice what you already have, blessings continue to expand.

When you are feeling positive and grateful, you attract more of what it is that you desire. Think about it. Consciously appreciating what you already have keeps you focused on abundance rather than on deficiency and deprivation. When you are envious, resentful, and constantly worried, you're focusing on failure. When you give fear, anxiety, and frustration top billing, you are creating a cycle of negativity that may take the shape of complaining to others while they attempt to out-complain you.

Research conducted by Robert Emmons, Ph.D., a professor of psychology at the University of California, Davis, and author of the books *Gratitude Works! A 21-Day Program for Creating Emotional Prosperity* and *Thanks! How the New Science of Gratitude Can Make You Happier,* has suggested that people who have high levels of gratitude have low levels of resentment and envy.

Positive focus is always more productive, and gratitude is a major component of that. We have also experienced that, when we are feeling and thinking positive thoughts, we draw positive people to us. We reflect off each other's attitudes, and it grows from there.

Abundance is not that picture-perfect six-bedroom house with a circular driveway and manicured lawns if the people who live there aren't happy. Abundance resides inside us. Abundance does not stem from "good luck." There are those who don't have enough to eat, and yet when they share with others what they do have, it ramps up their pleasure circuits and attracts reciprocal goodwill. When you are fully connected to gratitude for your (small or large) abode, and all the comforts you enjoy on a daily basis, you cannot help but enhance the beauty of your surroundings. Each time you give thanks for the people in your life, you are improving those relationships bit by bit. Gratitude will manifest abundance in all aspects of your life. Try it and see!

UNTIE THE DOCK LINES
AND LIVE YOUR DREAMS

It is not because things are difficult that we do not dare, it is because we do not dare that they are difficult.

—*Seneca*

NINA'S STORY

When my younger daughter, Jaime, was a senior in high school, I accompanied her to San Diego with another mother and daughter to tour local universities. Since the girls were not yet of drinking age, I went alone to a nearby bar that overlooked a gorgeous marina surrounded by lush tropical landscaping. The scene was so foreign to me, so Southern California. There was balmy weather, quite unlike the San Francisco Bay Area where we bundled up in layers year-round.

I gazed at the sailboats and motorboats, and felt like

someone on vacation in a faraway land—a vast cultural divide separated me from these people. I engaged in conversation with one of the boat owners, apparently a regular at this bar, who had recently returned from a fishing trip to Mexico.

Fish. I knew about fish! I ate seafood. While he talked about his recent catches, I listened, spellbound and in awe. My life was tied up with serious *responsibilities; it was completely impossible to imagine a leisurely pursuit like fishing from the deck of your very own blue-water boat! What an extraordinary concept. He then said something that has stayed with me all these years but which I completely dismissed at the time.*

He said, "Anyone can do this."

Anyone can buy a boat? Anyone can sail to Mexico and catch fish? That declaration, so seemingly farfetched at the time, has surfaced various times over the years, while its truth grew from impossibility, to a kernel of a dream, to an idea, and then into an action plan.

I attribute the transition from "it can't be done" to "maybe it IS possible" to "we DID it!" to the series of books Mary Beth and I co-wrote. After *Living Life as a Thank You* was published in 2009, we followed it up with *What Would You Do If You Knew You Could Not Fail?: How to Transform Fear into Courage.* For me, the process wasn't only researching, interviewing, and writing—I lived those books. Living and breathing gratitude transformed my life.

I noticed, and appreciated, that my life was improving in both small and big ways. As Sarah Ban Breathnach writes, "You simply will not be the same person two months from now after consciously giving thanks each day for the abundance that exists in your life. And you will have set in motion an ancient spiritual law: The more you have and are grateful for, the more will be given to you."

I fully related to people we interviewed, including Irina Lazar, who said, "Living in gratitude has become like a little game to me. I ask for things in life and then wait and see how they magically appear. Last night I said to myself that I needed a new caddy in my shower and a good Yoga class I could attend once a week. Now, I'm not wealthy—as a matter of fact, I am not earning money of any kind right now. This would normally stress people out, but I feel relaxed and grateful simply because my car works, I have a home, I have a life purpose and mission, I eat organic food every day, and I have a strong support system.

"I decided to take advantage of the beautiful day (and not having a job) and go for a hike. As I parked the car I saw that someone had left some free things out in front of their home for anyone to take, and there was a shower caddy in perfect condition sitting there waiting for me. I acknowledged this as the universe working in my favor and loaded it into my car. As I approached the entrance to the trail, I saw a Yoga class in the field with a sign that read "Free Yoga every day from 10:30–11:45 a.m." I noticed the free things and yoga because I am present; I notice what is going on around me because I know that, if I stay present, the world gives me presents!"

Every day, I worked on transforming my thoughts into positive ones, and I saw how I too received daily "presents," such as parking spots directly in front of venues, schedules that fell into place seamlessly, a 25-foot sailboat that was given to us when her owner got a job transfer overseas.

Two years later, when we wrote *What Would You Do If You Knew You Could Not Fail?*, it made me think deeply about what I was afraid of, and what was holding me back from living my life to the fullest. The book explores the concept of taking action—being afraid and doing "IT" anyway, whatever "IT" may be.

I addressed my fear of public speaking by enrolling in Toastmasters, which I wrote about in the book. During this time, my husband and I were taking sailing lessons, and we decided to buy a 27-foot sailboat with more bells and whistles to improve our skills. We talked about eventually buying a blue-water boat—a boat that was capable of ocean sailing—and taking her on long cruises. We couldn't really afford it, so we discussed the possibility of selling our home.

I was then faced with addressing a bigger fear—my

need for security. How could I sell my home, buy a sail-boat, say goodbye to everyone, and sail to the ends of the earth? It sounds wonderful, but is it safe? And yet here I was, advising others that, "You can make a choice to become more courageous. Ask yourself, 'Do I want to live out the rest of my life trying to be safe, or could I be brave enough to live out a fulfilling, exciting, and, yes, sometimes dangerous life?' It really is up to us and us alone to face our fears, and to honor them, and ourselves, so we can truly find peace and empowerment."

Sounds good—right? But was I ready to take my own advice?

I spent a lot of time fantasizing about my dream of sailing in tropical waters. Although I felt incredibly fortunate in my day-to-day life, I wanted to challenge myself further. I wanted adventure in my future, and sailing sounded like a perfect way to accomplish that.

I began to read everything I could get my hands on, and I found a common refrain in the advice given by seasoned sailors who had followed their passion and sailed to far-off places.

Many of them counseled, "If you want to sail away, do it today, don't wait." That advice doesn't seem to hold water for the many who can't afford it, or don't know how to sail. But I kept reading and learned that that a healthy bank account and decades of sailing experience are not the two most important things to start with. More important qualities are independence and an adventuresome spirit and, perhaps the most important quality, a belief in yourself and your dream.

I was also inspired by this quote from H. Jackson Brown Jr.: "Twenty years from now you will be more disappointed by the things that you didn't do than by the ones you did do. So throw off the bowlines. Sail away from the safe harbor. Catch the trade winds in your sails. Explore. Dream. Discover."

So we took the plunge. We found our dream boat for sale in Michigan, made an offer, and had *Silver Queen*, which we renamed *Gratitude*, transported to California. We didn't put our house on the market, but offered it for sale as a "pocket listing." The very next day, a buyer materialized and offered us more than full price, and we accepted.

As I write this, my husband and I are living on our boat and are in contract to buy another home, which we will rent out when we do our extended journey to the Sea of Cortez where we will be able to catch and prepare our own fish while we join the ranks of those living the dream. So yes, I guess that phrase, "anyone can do it," wasn't so preposterous, after all.

I credit the lessons I learned while writing *What Would You Do If You Knew You Could Not Fail?* and my daily practice of gratitude for inspiring me to untie my dock lines and follow my heart. My husband and I had virtually no experience when we decided we wanted to pursue a sailing lifestyle. But we knew these were learnable skills.

If someone like me, who had previously made all her decisions based on security and guarantees, could decide to sail off into the unknown, then I truly believe anyone can pursue their own dream. Or perhaps you are already living your dream, and the stories and practices in this book can help you further appreciate that truth.

Untie your lines—whatever they may be—and go for it!

GRATEFUL LIFE PRACTICE

My personal gratitude practice involves giving thanks all day. It's not hard at all.

If, like me, you have a tendency to think worrisome thoughts, begin to notice them and then offer yourself a counter-thought. For instance, if you are driving in your car, worried about being late, acknowledge that, but also give thanks that your car didn't choose that moment to break down. Thank you, car. It may set off a chain of grateful thoughts for the fact that we have the luxury of automobiles to take us places. If I am in critical mode with my children, I give thanks for the fact that they make *good* choices, even if they are different from the choices I might have made. This morning, since I am living at a marina, I went to the public restroom and found that it was occupied. Instead of grumbling about the hike I needed to take to the next rest stop, and all the other inconveniences of living at the marina, I turned that thought into one of appreciation for the fact that the restroom was almost always available. I focused on "the glass is half full," and it turned my hike into a pleasurable experience. This spilled over into my day. When I noticed how long the traffic light took to change from red to green, instead of giving way to impatience and irritation, I decided to focus on how fortunate we are to have traffic signals. During a recent visit to India, I witnessed how terrifying the alternative can be! I corral my thinking this way and consciously choose to append—if not replace entirely—an anxious thought with a grateful thought.

Yes, attaining an attitude of gratitude is something you have to work on, although I must say it's easily the most beneficial "work" I've ever performed.

THE CIRCLE OF LIFE: GRATITUDE BREEDS SUCCESS; SUCCESS BREEDS GRATITUDE

The greatest discovery of our generation is that human beings can alter their lives by altering their attitudes of mind. As you think, so shall you be.

—William James

In Los Angeles, Cheyann Benedict stands apart from many of the fit, attractive women sporting a casual look. For one, she is often credited with having created that "California casual" style when she, along with her former partner, Claire Stansfield, founded C&C California in 2003. Their high-end, luxurious knitwear line became an overnight success after it was featured in one of Oprah's famous "favorite things" episodes and was showcased in a Visa small-business commercial. Celebrities including Jennifer Aniston, Courtney Cox, and Sofia Coppola were seen around town wearing their comfortable T-shirts.

However, Cheyann's accomplishments were not handed to her. She credits her work ethic to her parents' edict that she could have anything in life but had to work very hard at whatever she did, and her artistic inspiration to her Cherokee background, her time spent in the early '80s Southern California punk rock scene, and the colorful sunsets she used to watch from the cliffs near her childhood home in San Diego.

As a teen Cheyann combed thrift stores for one-of-a-kind pieces that she recreated into original designs, eventually selling her custom styles to consignment stores in New York City to make extra money during university. She moved east to study theatre, attending the Experimental Theater Wing at NYU Tisch School of the Arts. After graduating she spent years doing avant-garde theater and postmodern dance off Broadway. Her fallback jobs were always in fashion, though, as it was hard to make a living doing "Art Theater." She took a position at the globally renowned boutique Calypso, where she expanded the brand to the West Coast. It was in Los Angeles that she met Claire Stansfield, and they founded the company that started the trend of T-shirts as a must-have fashion item.

Three years after the debut of their first collection, Cheyann and Claire sold C&C California to Liz Claiborne, and, not long after, Cheyann took off on a seven-year international journey that realigned her priorities *and clarified her purpose in life. Today, she mentors young women and helps others discover how to make their dreams come true. Her recently launched new venture, an eponymous clothing line, reflects her passion for authenticity and is inspired by her travels. Here, she shares what she learned along the way, and teaches us how to find— and trust—our inner voice.*

A self-described "road tripper," Cheyann has always enjoyed traveling. In 2006 she was so immersed in working that it was only after she fell in love with a man from New Zealand who traveled continuously for his work, that she was shocked out of her workaholic world. "There was something about his lifestyle that lit a spark for me," she says.

When Liz Claiborne purchased C&C in 2005, the founders agreed to act as co-presidents for five years, but after a year Cheyann realized that the corporate environment was not for her. She negotiated an early exit and hopped on a plane to India to travel the world. "When C&C was acquired I felt like I had done my job," she continues. "I had worked tirelessly to make it the success that it became, and I really felt like I was at a point where I needed to expand my life. I needed to grow and challenge myself in different ways."

For the next five months Cheyann "randomly" traveled through Europe and Asia, spontaneously choosing new destinations and experiencing total freedom. "To realize you could do that on a global scale was amazing," she says. "I took my time in each destination because the journey was mostly about getting to know myself." In Bangkok, she didn't leave her hotel for five days; she simply took the time to feel her feelings. It was there that she had an epiphany that "all the answers are within us—if we spend enough time asking ourselves the right questions, the answers will come." This realization is the quintessence of the message she imparts to the women she mentors who want to start fashion companies.

Cheyann also credits her daily practice of meditation with the shift in her consciousness and focus on stability. "After my travels I moved back to New York for three years," she continues. "I began studying different types of meditation, which led me to studying esoteric philosophy with Hugo Cory." (Hugo Cory developed the Natural Laws of Commerce to capture his belief that all we need to know about right work can be found in the wisdom of the natural world.) Cheyann says she learned how all good decisions come from a place of stability.

She also expresses her appreciation for connectivity— that she feels most grateful when she's experiencing connectivity to the people in her life, to the community, and most importantly, to herself. This deep thinker states that, when she's not thinking, she actually prefers "sharing and having a conversation," and that "encouraging others to live their dreams and know that they are awesome" is what makes her happiest.

When coaching aspiring entrepreneurs, Cheyann encourages each of them to really understand their underlying motivations. "We all have an emotional reason to do whatever we are doing," she says. "They might have an idea or a creative impulse, and I work with them to uncover their emotional space so they can gain clarity about what they really want, as opposed to what they think they want." She advises that it is critical to connect to our original inspiration when designing or creating art.

When Cheyann "messed up" in a business dealing, someone whose opinion she really valued gave her the impression that she was a "loser." "That lit a fire for me," she says, "and kick-started my motivation to show them what I can do. Sometimes anger is the fuel that gets us toward our destiny. Whatever it takes, don't judge it— work to become proud of yourself." She adds that the most important message is to be authentic and that "the only person who can make choices about you is YOU." That certainly applies to the origins of C&C, when the partners didn't listen to naysayers. "We were somewhat punk rock about it," she says. "If you are making things that others will say yes to, rather than what you say yes to, then that's not proper alignment."

Today she has a new clothing line made for women who are self-possessed, mobile, and interested in knowing themselves and the world around them. She is also proud that the line is made in the United States. "Sustainability is also found in taking care of our neighbors—and there is reverence in knowing where something is from," she adds.

GRATEFUL LIFE PRACTICE

Cheyann is rightly proud that the company she co-founded succeeded, despite the fact that so many fashion industry experts told her that what she was doing was wrong. Cheyann followed her intuition, her inner voice, and it paid off.

As the late Steve Jobs said in 2005, during a Stanford University commencement address, "Your time is limited, so don't waste it living someone else's life. Don't be trapped by dogma—which is living with the results of other people's thinking. Don't let the noise of others' opinions drown out your own inner voice. And most important, have the courage to follow your heart and intuition. They somehow already know what you truly want to become. Everything else is secondary."

If you are experiencing doubt about your path, or confusion about your next steps, you may want to print out some of the motivational quotes sprinkled throughout this book. Post them on your mirror or desktop computer or in your car to give you inspiration.

Here's another quote we like from one of the foremost

record producers of all time, Rick Rubin, who said, "I never decide if an idea is good or bad until I try it. So much of what gets in the way of things being good is thinking that we know. And the more that we can remove any baggage we're carrying with us, and just be in the moment, use our ears, and pay attention to what's happening, and just listen to the inner voice that directs us, the better."

BUILDING A FUTURE THROUGH THE SCHOOL OF HARD KNOCKS INSPIRES LIFELONG CAREER PASSION

Hem your blessings with thankfulness so they don't unravel.

—Unknown

As a designer and a single mom of two grown sons, Monarcha Marcet finds it inspiring to be in the realm of professionals who are focusing on providing aging-in-place services for clients at her Orlando-based Adventure in Building Inc.

Monarcha is at the pinnacle of her career doing a job she loves and, at the same time, making a difference. She is meeting a growing desire of Americans to stay put—aging in place is the popular term—by renovating their houses so they can be user-friendly and safe for their aging selves. In the fall of 2013, she was honored for her efforts by the National Association of Home Builders.

But her dream job and meaningful life were learned through the School of Hard Knocks. After graduating from college and marrying an architect, Monarcha got pregnant and had two sons within two years. There were signs of trouble along the way, as she gave up pieces of herself, made compromises, and slowly let go of her dreams and career aspirations as she made compromises to try to hold her family together. After her sons were born, she also quit her job to become a full-time mother. "My creativity all went into my sons," she says. "They had the most elaborate birthday parties you could ever imagine."

When her sons went off to school, she went back to work, launching her own design and building firm. But in 1980s, when the recession dried up the building industry, her husband's business hit a wall and things got very stressful for the family. Though the couple worked for years on their marriage, seeking counseling help and trying to hang in there, Monarcha became severely depressed in 1995 and attempted to take her own life. After being hospitalized, and receiving individual counseling, she realized one thing: "I'm either going to be here on this earth, or I am going to be married." The couple divorced.

"Though it was a very painful time, I am very grateful that that happened, because it gave me the perspective to make that decision and to fight to recover my life," she

says. "My sons were young teens and very angry, but I had to reconnect with who I was and reconnect with my dreams."

In the midst of transition, Monarcha hung on, as the eye of the divorce sent her world spinning. At one point she had to short-sell her home. She also underwent four shoulder surgeries, and the financial challenge of having to support two sons through high school and college created seemingly relentless stress.

But somehow, she says, she survived and thrived. Today her son Sebastian is 30, her son Christopher is 28, and all is well. Here, Monarcha speaks frankly about the strength she found on her journey and how blessed she says she feels.

As a child, Monarcha trailed her father on his job as a construction value estimator, and in high school she fell in love with drafting classes, aspiring to one day become an architect. "I remember my expression used to be that something was good if it made your heart sing," says Monarcha. "The idea that I could be an architect made my heart sing."

But when it was time for college she chose interior decorating, "because that is what girls did." The good news was that the beginning design classes she was taking were the same for a building degree, so she could aim higher and design the whole building, not just decorate the inside.

As one of only three females in her major, she earned a four-year bachelor of design in architecture degree from the University of Florida. After her graduation, she spent a summer on Nantucket Island learning preservation, and landed a job with an architect doing the construction measurements for a prominent historic preservation project. She was on fire with passion for building and design, and for making her dreams come true.

At the same time she began dating an architect and got married. During the first year of her marriage, she went back to University of Florida for a master of building construction degree. "Because two architects in one family might lead to divorce, I decided I'd be better as a building contractor," she says, but, as she looks back now, "it was the first in a long series of events where I started to give up my dream."

The couple moved to Boston, where they lived for two years. Monarcha got pregnant and they moved back to Florida. "I was probably the only pregnant woman taking the contractor's exam. (I wore a great T-shirt that had an arrow pointing down that said, 'under construction.')" But to avoid marital problems, she put her career on hold and helped her husband reach his career goals, becoming a full-time mom until the boys were in pre-school. Then she started her company, Adventure in Building, but a move to another city for her husband's job created a challenge of starting over.

Fast-forward, as the marriage woes mounted and the stress of the economy on the construction industry led to Monarcha's severe depression, a very complicated and nasty divorce, and the challenges that followed, raising her sons solo. It wasn't until after the divorce that her dreams and the company were able to reignite.

Some might see her story as one of giving up and giving in, but, with each roadblock, she says she focused on the positive and the blessings that were there for her at the time. Focusing on what she was thankful for begot more blessings, and all along the way the challenges turned into opportunities.

Through the challenge, Monarcha also found spiritual strength. Though she doesn't currently attend any church regularly, she says, "I went on a pilgrimage of sorts during my depression time and found a charismatic movement that was having manifestations of the Holy Spirit," and she was transformed. During her quest, she laughs, "I also learned that God has a sense of humor. A godly friend said I could ask God for a sign that I was loved. I said if I saw three rainbows in one day that would be a sign for me. Along with seeing real rainbows the next day, I was writing checks and laid out three checks on the table. My checks had rainbows on them, and when I looked down at them I laughed out loud."

On her spiritual journey, she changed the spelling of her first name from Manarcha to Monarcha, to symbolize the new life, the transformation like a butterfly, that she feels God blessed her with.

"For the last 18 years, I feel like I've been in a cocoon and that I am only just starting to emerge," she says. "I've had challenges too, like four shoulder surgeries in a two-year time frame. I had to short-sell my house. I had to work part-time for a major building consumer store. But I know I am loved by God for sure, and that is what keeps me going."

In the end, when she asks herself, "What is the meaning of life?" she thinks of something she heard from a Kurt Vonnegut book: "to be the eyes and ears and conscience of the creator of the universe." She adds, "I also say something my counselor told me: 'Success is the best revenge.' What we tell ourselves is how we live."

GRATEFUL LIFE PRACTICE

For Monarcha, showing her gratitude daily involves a prayer ritual: "I pray always, always." She says she starts each day ready to reset and refresh, but offering a prayer of gratitude for that day. Do you have a favorite quote or prayer? Keep a copy on your bedside as a "prayer prompter" to express your gratitude every day.

FALLING ASLEEP, GRATEFULLY

Before bed each night, Holly Sammons takes time to review her day and to review the gifts she received. It's a practice she started to stave off the insomnia or middle-of-the-night awakenings when she couldn't get herself back to sleep.

Instead of lying in bed tossing and turning and churning, she started using the gratitude alphabet.

Here's how she says it works: Start with the letter "A" and think of something you're grateful for that begins with A. Then on to B, and work your way through the alphabet.

"I have never, in over 20 years of doing the gratitude alphabet, gotten to letter Z. I've always fallen asleep long before getting very far in the alphabet," she says. "I think it changes the restless, sleepless mind to a quiet calm place, ready and open to sleep."

Indeed, according to one of our favorite gratitude-inspiring go-to sites, www.DailyOm.com, "When we have good days, we often find ourselves going over the details later, enjoying them a second and third time as we feel the joy of our good fortune. When we have bad days, we may find ourselves poring over the details of our misfortunes. However, we can reframe those bad days by making it a daily practice to spend some time before going to bed each night to review the gifts we received that day. Regardless of our evaluation of the day—good, bad, mediocre—we can call forth the many blessings that were present. This practice transforms our consciousness as it reveals the fullness at the heart of our lives."

Caveat: Be patient with yourself as you begin this practice. We're wired to stress over the worrisome experiences, so we need to dig deeper to recount the gifts. You can keep it simple and focus on the basics—you have a roof over your head, or you have people in your life who bring you joy.

With practice, your bedtime gratefulness practice can help you focus on the gifts of the day and have a restful sleep. "Nighty-night and sweet dreams."

CHAPTER NINE
FINDING GRATITUDE IN THE EVERYDAY

*Trade your expectation for appreciation and the
world changes instantly.*

—Tony Robbins

Why is it that we're always looking for that "something
more" in our lives and are never fully satisfied with what
we have? It seems we're always hoping that someone or
something else will make our lives better. Sometimes we
forget to take time to recognize the blessings that are
already defining our lives. Maybe it's because we've become
so habituated to focusing on the messages we encounter
during each day about what we don't have, instead of
the blessings and abundance that are already there. This
conflict can leave us feeling drained, empty, and isolated.

But before turning to a prescription medication to relieve

feelings of anxiety, try identifying and then changing your thought processes when experiencing a "trigger moment," or inner turmoil. We've demonstrated throughout this book that replacing images of bad outcomes with grateful thoughts is linked to decreases in depression and anxiety. This makes perfect sense: By sparking positive thoughts in the prefrontal cortex, fear circuits are soothed. There's an old saying that if you've forgotten the language of gratitude, you'll never be on speaking terms with happiness.

To honor the blessings in our lives, we have to be purposeful about recognizing the richness that is woven into the everyday of our lives. In many ways, our search is about surfacing the unseen more than the visible, which is why finding the gratitude in your everyday life is often a spiritual process of enlightenment. In this chapter, we share the stories of ordinary people who were leading comparatively insular lives, not fully understanding or appreciating the blessings in their lives—that is, until they stopped and looked closely at those who were walking alongside them. Then they were able to tap into the full scope of prosperity that comes from our shared journey with others who bring blessings into our lives.

These awakenings, and paying attention to the blessings that happen every moment through the course of their days, opened their hearts to a flood of compassionate gratitude. Now, inside every day, they live with a deeper level of gratitude that allows them to bask in and appreciate their lives with a renewed sense of hope. Our hope is that these stories will help you rise every day to recognize the abundance that surrounds you. In the words of Walt Whitman: "As for me, I know of nothing else but miracles."

TWIN BLESSINGS: GRATITUDE LEADS TO PEACE, WHICH LEADS TO FULFILLMENT

Write it on your heart that every day is the best day in the year.

—Ralph Waldo Emerson

As so often happens in a life lived with gratitude, like-minded people meet, virtually or in person, and find that they have much in common. This happened to this book's co-author, Nina Lesowitz, when she reached out to southern Rhode Island resident Laura Rossi, 44, after reading an article by Brian Alexander in the June 2013 issue of MORE *magazine. Titled "Change One Habit, Change Your Life," the article highlights how Laura fostered a habit of gratitude to help her change her habits. After talking, both women discovered that their lives have followed similar trajectories—beginning as English majors and continuing on career paths as consumer public relations professionals and book publicists, and also in their personal lives as mothers of two children, recreational sailors (on opposite coasts), and gratitude practitioners.*

A graduate of the University of Connecticut, Laura spent a decade in New York City. She met her husband, Randy, an avid sailor, when she participated in a Newport-to-Block-Island regatta. They married in 1999, and in 2003 she became pregnant with twins. Her boy and girl were both born healthy, but several weeks later her son had to have surgery. According to Laura, that "opened up a Pandora's Box of problems which was compounded by the fact that he wasn't gaining weight. From birth he was subjected to a whole batch of genetic tests and diagnoses, and it was very hard and confusing."

He is now 10 years old, and occupational therapists have been working with him on his fine motor skills, gross motor skills, and related issues. Recently, the family received a diagnosis of Sensory Processing Disorder (SPD) and some other issues. SPD is a neurological disorder causing difficulties with taking in, processing, and responding to sensory information about the environment and from within one's own body.

Although it was a relief to finally get a diagnosis, that wasn't what alleviated Laura's high level of stress and worry. Laura was only able to change her outlook from "the glass is always half empty" to one of joy and appreciation through a dedicated practice of visualization and a habit of gratitude.

A self-described "recovering perfectionist," Laura titled her blog "My So-Called Sensory Life" because of her son's diagnosis. She is a frequent Huffington Post columnist and avid blogger; her blog was named a "2011 Top 25 Most Inspiring Families Blog" by Circle of Moms. But Laura didn't set out to write about her trials and tribulations as the mother of twins, including one with special needs. Instead, she used her blog as a forum to describe one blessing every day or, as Laura describes it, "to celebrate the silver lining (the 'gift') we can find every day—especially on the tough days." Laura committed to writing one blog post every single day for 365 consecutive days, with the goal of preserving and capturing a year of unexpected daily gifts from motherhood.

It wasn't long after she began blogging in March 2010 that she noticed her daily commitment—whether she was on a deadline, on a business trip, or sick with the flu—had begun to transform her outlook.

Laura describes herself in the early years of motherhood, when she was "a wreck, going on adrenalin, and was usually in a state of panic," while her husband, who is more pragmatic, would counsel her to "stay in the moment." But Laura couldn't do that. Her automatic response was to "catastrophize" every incident. If she got a call from school, she would immediately assume the worst. She bemoaned how far her life strayed from her expectations; a self-described "Type A" personality, Laura wasn't emotionally prepared to deal with so much confusion and fear. "I still have that kind of energy—I am very anal about deadlines," she laughs. "But I have a different calmness, a sense of joy, and my mood and priorities have undergone a complete transformation. Maybe I needed this challenge to take it down a notch?" A strong believer in fate, Laura says, "My husband Randy and I feel like we've been chosen for this. Each of us is given what we can handle, and I feel so lucky and blessed to have a special-needs child who has helped me become a better person on so many levels."

Laura says she has learned so much from her son. "I had an epiphany one day when I was observing one of his weekly therapy sessions," she says. "He was learning techniques about turning off bad feelings, and I realized I could do the very same thing: Start over. Start new. Forget what just happened. It's like having the ability to hit a 'refresh' button. I realized that you can dictate how your day will go by your attitude." One of the techniques Laura employed was to visualize: "In my mind, I pictured a light switch, and then I would imagine turning off the light switch, and I'd say to myself, 'I can do this.' If it's hard, or I'm scared, I would say to myself: 'I'm a grownup, I can do this, I am strong.' "

As the mother of a special-needs child, she's been exposed to her share of negativity on the part of other, less conscious parents. "I take a two-pronged approach to negativity," she explains. "First of all, I am honest with myself. If my child isn't invited to a birthday party, or if I overhear a parent complain that my child is slowing down her child's progress in class, I work through it by discussing it with my mother and sister, with whom I am very close. Then I employ my mantra: 'Forget about it; move on; you get what you get and don't get upset!' I make a list of what I'm grateful for, and soon enough I realize that it's not about me, it's about the other person. Eventually, I feel compassion for him or her.

Today Laura feels like she's exactly where she needs to be in her life. When others offer sympathy for her responsibilities as the mother of her precious son, she always responds by exclaiming how lucky she is.

GRATEFUL LIFE PRACTICE

Laura is often asked about her other twin, and, as all parents of more than one child know, sometimes it feels like one gets more attention than the other. Laura and Randy work hard to treat the children equally, but it can be harder with twins because they are fiercely competitive for attention, especially when one has special needs or challenges. Here is Laura's response: "We are a diverse family—all of us have strengths and challenges, just like every other family. For us, we navigate things in real time, and I always try to narrate situations so that they become teachable moments for my daughter and my son. I always highlight the positive for both children and emphasize how very lucky we all are to have one another."

We are including one of Laura's blog postings, because it describes a practice that we often recommend: Take the time today to really see your child, or your spouse, or your parent through grateful eyes, and you will notice an immediate effect that will have long-term benefits.

Laura writes: *My blog focuses on M, but, because they are twins, I often find that I can't write about him without writing about her. They shape and influence and complement one another in so many ways.*

Today, though, is J's day. I step back and admire, appreciate and love her for the amazing person she is. J has a huge heart. J is a deeply sensitive, emotional girl. She is also passionate and colorful and dramatic and artistic. She is kind and caring. She is smart and beautiful. J is patient. She loves to dance and sing and loves reading and math and school. She is a loyal friend and a great student. She's an amazing and incredible daughter, granddaughter, and cousin. And she is the best sister anyone could want. She's a dream come true—literally.

J is growing up beautifully, though sometimes my

heart aches because things can be hard because of M's needs (though she never complains).

Today I celebrate the gift of my daughter with as much joy as the day I met her.

CULTIVATING GRATITUDE FOR YOU

We have been focusing on expressing gratitude for those around us and being thankful for the many opportunities and gifts bestowed on us by others. Now we ask that you take some time to see the good in yourself, and then give thanks for the qualities that you admire about YOU! When you look in the mirror, do you immediately notice a flaw? It is hard not to do this, since we are surrounded by messages of self-improvement. What if, instead, you looked in the mirror and concentrated on something you like about your reflection? And then took that one step further, by taking pen to paper and listing 10 things you like about yourself?

You can list physical attributes, accomplishments, and aspects of your character that would roll off your tongue if you were complimenting a good friend. Ever notice that we often downplay the good that we do, while simultaneously holding another person on a pedestal for the Exact Same Thing? "Oh, volunteering for the animal shelter is

nothing, really. I feel so guilty that I don't go more often."
Yet, we consider others saintly for doing the same thing.

Today, let's turn this tendency around by countering
that inner critic. After you've listed those 10 attributes or
qualities, carry the list around with you. Every time you
find yourself in belittlement mode, take out the list and
read it to yourself. Or make a mental note, and counter
each criticism with something positive.

For instance, when you begin to give yourself a hard
time for your weight, quickly exchange that thought with
one of gratitude for your sense of style. Or if the thought
enters your head that you are a terrible cook, or never got
around to learning a second language, or spent too much
of your income last month, or...or..., then answer it thus:
"Yes, but I did drive my friend to the hospital / make a
roomful of people laugh / walk my dog for an hour today."
Not only will your self-esteem benefit, but you will experience an increase in satisfaction with your life as a whole.

You'll also be better equipped for the other gratitude
practices in this book. When it comes to self-appreciation,
charity does begin at home.

WIRED FOR HAPPINESS: APPLICATIONS TO INCREASE YOUR GRATITUDE QUOTIENT

Cultivate the habit of being grateful for every good thing that comes to you, and give thanks continuously. And because all things have contributed to your advancement, you should include all things in your gratitude.

—Ralph Waldo Emerson

Since the publication of our book *Living Life as a Thank You* in 2009, there has been a proliferation of apps for your iPhone that make it easy to begin—and maintain—a gratitude practice. According to Benny Hsu, 35, a Jacksonville, Florida-based app developer, blogger (getbusylivingblog. com) and creator of the Gratitude 365 app, "We're so used to having our iPhone with us from the time we wake up till the time we go to bed," he says. "Having a way to quickly write and keep your gratitudes in one place was the reason I wanted to create this app. No need for a journal that you might forget where you put it." His app enables users to add a photo to each day and has a calendar view so they can view their photos in an organized way.

Benny was inspired to develop a gratitude app after experiencing a lack of meaning in his life. A graduate of the University of Florida with a degree in sports management, Benny looked for jobs related to sports in the front office, but in Jacksonville the opportunities were limited. So he began working at the family restaurant. The plan was to just work there until he could figure out what he wanted to do. Living and working with his parents, he started off clearing tables, and worked his way up to manager. Benny was making good money now, drove a BMW, and bought a house. But he never intended this life—so he continued to try to figure out what else he wanted to do.

"Late 2010 was a huge turning point in my life. That's when I decided to take responsibility for everything in my life. I did not like the type of person I had become. I felt like I was sleepwalking through life," he says. "I was in a job I hated and had been stuck there for the past five years. I had no idea what other type of job I wanted to do either. I couldn't just quit because I had bills to pay. I was frustrated and just hated everything about my life. If you didn't know me, you would have thought my life was perfect from the outside. I had everything I could possibly want, but so much was missing from my life.

"I knew about the power of gratitude for a long time, but never applied it. I always focused on what I didn't have and what I wished I had. I wasn't happy at all, so how could I be grateful for anything? I had done what I was supposed to do in life. I got good grades in school, got a job out of college, made good money, and bought a house.

"When I decided to take back control of my life, I knew I needed to do everything differently. The thoughts, choices, beliefs, and actions I had taken up to that point were not getting me the results I wanted. So it was important that I change. I didn't want the next five years to be like the past five. I decided to keep a gratitude journal because it was something I had never done. I knew how much it has helped others, and I knew I needed to change my mindset. So I wrote in a gratitude journal every morning. I just listed 10 things I was grateful for. I made it part of my morning routine."

With no programming experience, Benny created his first iPhone app, Photo 365. He hired a team to create it, and it was released in August 2011. In the first 30 days it was featured by Apple as App of the Week and earned over $30,000.

Even more important, Benny says, "I changed as a person. I grew up. I finally felt excited about my future. I had direction in my life and didn't feel stuck anymore. I truly believe I achieved so much that year because I changed on the inside first. Gratitude helped shift my focus to appreciate what I already had. I began to see opportunities and not closed doors." So naturally, his next app was designed around the concept of gratitude.

Benny's Gratitude 365 app is designed to help others—especially younger people who are accustomed to using their iPhones to manage their lives—find meaning and achieve lasting happiness.

GRATEFUL LIFE PRACTICE

If you have a smart phone, try downloading one of the many apps available today. Even if you don't use it regularly, just seeing the icon on your phone screen will remind you to think of something positive today, and will connect you to others throughout the cyber universe who are using the power of gratitude to make their dreams come true.

Here are just a few. You can find them by entering either the name of the app or the developer in the search area of iTunes:

The Gratitude Journal from Happy Tapper

Live Happy by Signal Patterns

Thankfulfor by Shiny Heart Ventures

And on Google Play, there is an Android app, Attitudes of Gratitude Journal, by Vista Play, and My Gratitude Journal by KDC Global.

RANDOM ACTS OF PIZZA: DELIVERIES OF HOPE TO A YOUNG CANCER PATIENT

Real friendship or love is not manufactured or achieved by an act of will or intention. Friendship is always an act of recognition.

—John O'Donohue

Customers love the pizza-by-the-slice at Pizza Bella in Palatine, Illinois, but the menu item that keeps nine-year-old Rosie Colucci coming back isn't edible. It's the big-hearted bear hug delivered by owner Tony De Filippis and the playful banter that leaves both laughing and smiling. "You can't help but smile knowing Rosie," says De Filippis about one of his most frequent, and admittedly "favorite" customers.

Her at-least-twice-a-week visits are a reminder of what a determined and courageous young girl with a devoted family can achieve. Rosie and her "Wingman" (mom) and big sister Bella spend hours brewing new and creative philanthropic ideas and/or discussing Rosie's latest charities with Tony. "She's an unstoppable fund-raiser," smiles De Filippis. "All she does is think about ways she can help other sick kids, whether it's promoting blood donation, collecting unused medical supplies, collecting new toys, or raising funds for research, Rosie's heart and soul is all about giving back."

When he learned that his regular pint-sized customer was fighting brain cancer, he was moved to action to help ease the financial burden of the medical bills for her parents, and to do more. Always supporting all she does, on Rosie's sixth birthday and regularly since then De Filippis has delivered regular "pizza on the house" to Rosie and her family. During Rosie's "Celebration of Life" party, which included family, friends, and "the whole neighborhood" of 100 to 150 people at the Colucci house, Tony made sure there was enough food to go around. "Every day should be a celebration of life," Rosie's mom, JoAnne, says.

Rosie, nine, now a fourth grader, was officially diagnosed with neurofibromatosis or NF1 on her third birthday. The genetic disorder causes tumors to grow in and on the nerves throughout the body. Rosie was thought to have the disorder after an early well visit to the doctor when she was just six months old. Within weeks of her third birthday and NF diagnosis, Rosie was

*diagnosed with not one but two life-threatening condi-
tions—an inoperable brain tumor and Acquired Obstruc-
tive Hydrocephalus. She now suffers from a half-dozen
other chronic conditions, with multiple tumors in her
brain as well, making her case extremely rare and complicated. Since 2007, she has had almost 200 doses of chemo,
16 surgeries, and countless tests and procedures. She sees
13 specialists at Lurie Children's Hospital in Chicago,
and she has missed over 150 days of school since she
started treatment. Rosie, whose favorite color is "tie-die
and rainbows," was nicknamed "Rock Star Rosie" by her
nurses at the hospital. Rosie calls Children's her second
home. "It's my hospital," says Rosie, who says she was
moved to try to do something to make other kids smile.*

Hospitals can be boring, depressing places, especially
when you're a kid. Rosie knows this firsthand. But the
smell of pizza and the unexpected friendship of Tony, "the
pizza guy," speak volumes about how small gestures of
kindness—or call them "Random Acts of Pizza"—can
cushion life's toughest blows in huge ways.

Tony will never forget the day four years ago when he
was in his office and one of his employees told him that
there was a little girl at the counter, and he just had to
come out and meet her.

The little girl was Rosie, and she was asking for a
donation to help other kids with cancer, Tony remembers.

"When you meet Rosie, you'd never know she was sick, she's so filled with life and always so positive," he says.

The duo became fast friends. They have an almost brother-and-sister-like friendship, with lots of teasing and joking around. Since then, Rosie; her sister, Bella; and her mom, JoAnne, have become at least twice-a-week regulars at Pizza Bella.

Since meeting Rosie, Tony has helped stage many "Celebration Toy Drives" for Rosie's Toy Box, a charity that collect toys, books, and games to donate to Lurie Children's Hospital. Tony and Pizza Bella also hold "Cupcakes for Kids" specials in which one dollar of each cupcake sale goes to the children's hospital, and he's helped Rosie collect unused medical supplies for mission trips.

"I think we're put in contact with certain people for a reason," says Tony. "Rosie came into my life to help me learn to relax and not take life for granted."

"Tony and Rosie have inspired each other," says JoAnne. "When Rosie's sick, she knows people like Tony are there for her and care about her."

Rosie says she is dedicating her life to "spreading sunshine, joy, and hope" to other kids. She started Rosie's Toy Box when she was just four years old. It is dedicated to raising awareness for pediatric brain cancer and collecting new toys for the children's hospital.

Rosie says, "My hospital stays were sometimes boring. I noticed the other kids needed things to do. One visit, I got so many toys, I said to my mom, 'I can't keep all these.' I wanted to give back to the other kids. That's how Rosie's Toy Box started."

"Rosie has taught me to take every day and cherish it," says Tony, 31. "She is someone who might not get to experience everything that life has to offer, and that has made me realize that the little things in life are the most important. Rosie makes me take a step back to enjoy the things that most people would overlook on a day-to-day basis. To have a little girl who just finished a chemo treatment come in and be excited to show me a rainbow outside really puts things into perspective."

GRATEFUL LIFE PRACTICE

Since meeting Rosie, Tony has made it a practice to nurture his relationships with the community and give back. He recommends investigating organizations in your community where you could make a difference and volunteering to help as an expression of your gratefulness.

CHAPTER TEN

THE SECRET TO A GRATITUDE MAKEOVER: HOW TO CREATE GRATITUDE PRACTICES THAT STICK

Ninety-nine percent of the time we have an opportunity to be grateful for something. We just don't notice it. We go through our days in a daze."

—David Steindl-Rast, O.S.B.

From challenges to triumphs, gratitude is not just a word, it is a way of life. If you're in the mood for a change in your life, big or small, you've come to the right place. We're celebrating what lies ahead by celebrating the stories of the people in this book who speak volumes about our belief that there is no better way to create abundance in your life than through being grateful for what you have right now.

You're still asking, "Why should I say thank you when... I just lost my job, my husband walked out, or there's some other challenge that feels horrible right now?" We know, we've been there, and so have many of the people we talked to who have suffered significant health challenges, devastating destruction, and life challenges that seem daunting. But, they've shown us the power of saying thank you because you know there is a rainbow waiting on the other side, that you can rebuild, and you can come out on the other side of whatever hurdle or setback you are facing. So say thank you right now, knowing you are walking through and you will get to the other side. You're saying thank you because you are living in the hope of that.

Expect to smile, laugh, cry, and experience a new journey when you infuse your life with thankfulness. It starts by paying attention to the blessings in your daily life and cultivating gratitude practices that help you focus on what you have now and how thankful you are for everything that has shown up in your life.

According to the *Journal of American Psychology*, people who kept a "gratitude diary" for nine weeks felt happier and healthier, and even exercised more.

Still skeptical? Sure, you're saying, we'd all love to create good feelings of gratitude in our daily lives—if only we knew how. We understand that talking about gratitude, and savoring it, is easier said than done. Cultivating gratefulness and an appreciation of every day, especially in the midst of loss, is a learned practice. It happens over time. Just like training for a running race, or learning to ride a bike, play the piano, or practice meditation and yoga, frequency and a commitment to practicing gratitude are very important. It takes practice and honing your skills. Don't expect perfection, but know that practice and dedication can help you refocus your outlook on life, and that it creates permanence by ingraining the habit of gratitude into your daily living.

There are many reasons to be grateful. In the November 2013 issue of Oprah magazine, comedian Margaret Cho expresses gratitude for her thighs: "It's hard to find peace with your thighs, but when they chafe, try to be grateful for them. Your thighs let you run and get you where you want to go. I have not just thigh peace but thigh happiness, and it begins with thigh gratitude."

In this chapter we share what we've learned about starting a gratitude practice and staying in a state of thankfulness. Once you start focusing on what you have and how thankful you are for what you have, you will notice everything that starts showing up in your life.

We're hoping to inspire you and to help you understand why it is so important to pay attention to the blessings in your life. We don't have all the answers, but we want to join the challenge with you. We're hoping that by doing this collectively, we will have a broader impact that ripples across the country and the world. We're trying to walk the walk, and we're starting small too. The first step is noticing. Instead of asking, "What did you do today that makes you grateful?" we started asking ourselves, "What did you notice today that was a blessing, what small gift came into your life today?" By paying attention to the moment-by-moment experiences in our lives that we notice at any given time—a door held open for you when you walk into the coffee shop, a kind word from a co-worker, an extra hug from your child, etc.—we shape what stands out to us, and the grudges, fears, and stress fade into the background. We promise that, if you seize the moments and start noticing the important details that are right in front of us, we invite reflection on what is good and what blessings in our lives resonate with us.

JIMMY FALLON'S HILARIOUS
THANK YOU LETTERS

Every Friday is Thanksgiving for Jimmy Fallon. If you roll your eyes at some of the traditional "thank you" cards, consider these original thoughts from Jimmy Fallon:

- Thank you, people who wear full-length down coats, for showing me what it would look like if sleeping bags had legs.
- Thank you, winter hats that look like cute animals, for allowing guys who wear you to stay warm and single at the same time.
- Thank you, pita bread, for being a great combination between wheat and envelopes.
- Thank you, people who say the phrase, "I really shouldn't," for letting me know you're about to eat a lot of my fries.

TRAINS, POSTCARDS AND CYBERSPACE—ONE WOMAN LAUNCHES "THE GRATITUDE PROJECT: DARE TO BE GRATEFUL" MOVEMENT

Wherever gratitude goes, gratitude grows.

—Jo-Anne Guimond, founder of "The Gratitude
Project"

Jo-Anne Guimond is daring to be grateful. In 2013, after realizing how many blessings she had in her life, and how closely they were intertwined with others, she wondered if others also found themselves "swimming in gratitude." Her question "Wouldn't it be cool to find out what others are grateful for?" sparked the idea for "The Gratitude Project: Dare to be Grateful."

It *started with a train trek across Canada and blossomed into a multi-faceted initiative that evolved into the blog, community events, travel, story collecting, a postcard project, and charitable fund-raising.*

The Ottawa resident launched "The Gratitude Project," on a 2,626.8-mile train trip from Toronto to Vancouver. A natural introvert, the blogger wore her "What are you grateful for?" T-shirt to engage other passengers and to collect their stories en route.

She chronicled the experience on social media—Facebook and Twitter—and, beyond cyberspace, she brought the project into the community. Starting at the train's first stop in Arts Park in Ottawa's Hintonburg neighborhood, she set up a table and, at stops along the way, dropped off stamped, self-addressed post cards asking people to share what they were grateful for.

"One of the most moving moments was when a woman answered the question, 'Which person whom you haven't met are you most grateful for?' by saying, 'My daughter's birth mother.' "

Jo-Anne framed the question differently for kids, asking them, "What are you happy about?" One of the sweetest responses from the under-10 set was, "I'm happy that my mom loves me... How do you spell mom?"

The response to "The Gratitude Project" surpassed all Jo-Anne's expectations. It became contagious. During the course of her three-and-a-half day train trek, more than a dozen travelers stepped forward to share their gratitude stories, which she chronicled on her blog. In addition, she received more than 50 postcards from people who found them at her drop-off spots across the train journey. (Some

even found their way to Ireland, she's not sure how.)
Inspired by the project on cyberspace, 39 guest bloggers
answered the question, "What are you grateful for?" And
249 followers "liked" the project and formed an online
community on Facebook. Almost 200 people contributed
to four community events that were held.

The movement also touched the younger genera-
tion when Jo-Anne took it to classrooms. Eighth-grade
students penned more than a dozen essays on gratitude.
A couple of dozen people supported the project early
on by purchasing the limited-edition T-shirts that were
produced, and promoted it every time they wore it!

"I know there are similar projects that have much
bigger numbers, but that was never my goal," Jo-Anne
says. "Every time the project got a 'like' on Facebook or
a new follower on Twitter, and if it was a name I did
not know, I was giddy. The fact that this project rippled
beyond my small known world was absolutely thrilling."

It was January 2013 when Jo-Anne found herself basking
in the sun poolside in South Beach, Fla. She had just
completed her goal—the Miami Half-Marathon—and
was reflecting on how grateful she was for her health. "For
an Ottawa girl, being in warm Florida in January alone
was enough to be grateful for," she says.

Months earlier, she and her husband had sold their
house and bought a "perfect-for-us" loft in a vibrant

Ottawa neighborhood. "I still have 'pinch-me' moments about that," says Jo-Anne, who works full time managing the learning and programs unit for the Library of Parliament in their human resources department. "It all happened quite quickly, when we weren't really looking to buy / sell, and it couldn't have gone more smoothly. Our house sale allowed us to reach some financial goals that were initially seven to eight years into the future."

The move also forced the couple to "get rid of a lot of stuff" that simply wasn't serving them anymore. She remembers feeling "light and lean." She adds, "Also, I had two major trips planned for 2013." One was the solo train journey, a long-held dream of hers; the other was travelling to Europe with her husband, who was registered to run the Berlin Marathon. They had decided to combine that trip with a short visit to Paris and London. "I mean really, how does one get so blessed?"

Indeed, she says the blessings were overflowing, prompting her idea to reach outside herself and discover what others were grateful for.

"At first, I saw this as something I would do during my train trip across Canada—but it evolved," she says. "I incorporated the concept of 'daring' in the title of the project because I truly do believe it is an act of daring. It seems so many people find it easier to blame and complain. It takes intention—and yes, daring—to go beyond that and see the gifts our reality is holding out for us to see.

This doesn't mean that all is pretty and perfect. Grateful people are no Pollyannas—we are simply people who are perhaps willing to reach a little deeper to find meaning in our lives."

At the beginning, Jo-Anne just hoped to engage people in gratitude conversation during the train trek. "I am essentially an introvert, and I knew I could easily spend that time alone," she says. "And that would have been okay. But I wanted something different for this trip. I wanted to s-t-r-e-t-c-h. One of the very first images that popped into my mind was me, wearing a T-shirt that said, "What are you grateful for?"

Since it was uncomfortable for her to start conversations with strangers, the T-shirt helped her put the conversation out there and hope that fellow train riders would come to her. She set up four goals:

1. To express and share her personal gratitude with others
2. To reach out and engage others—friends and strangers—in a conversation around gratitude
3. To inspire others to put their gratitude into action
4. To step out of her comfort zone and learn

It was the stories about being grateful—in good times and challenging ones—that brought Jo-Anne the most joy from the project. The messages were infused with thankfulness for health, faith, and family, and for things large and small—the smile of a person on the street, the tip left by a customer, a cup of coffee to start the day, and the ability to spend time with an aging parent.

"One of the postcards I received said, 'Today I dare to be grateful for…the ability to walk and run again without pain," she says. "This one really speaks to me because I will be running my first marathon in 2014 and often find it challenging to stay motivated."

She adds, "So many people shared about being grateful for their families—children, aging parents, siblings. This helped me become even more appreciative of my family, many of whom don't live close by. I am now making a more intentional effort to contact them more often."

The guest bloggers were beyond generous with their sharing. "Time and time again, "Jo-Anne says, "I was overcome when I would read their submissions. One of them that really surprised me was the person who wrote that she was grateful for the medical condition that was killing her. Talk about a depth of gratitude."

Hearing the gifts others were grateful for in their lives, Jo-Anne reminded herself of how grateful she was for her spiritual life. "A God beyond my understanding works and creates through me every day," she says. "I am in God, and God is in me. I don't need to preach it or prove it. It just is. And everything else flows from there… And for that I am most grateful."

Though the program was slated to end at the close of 2013, Jo-Anne is not putting an official ending to it and will let it wind down (or—who knows?—grow) organically.

Already, she has surpassed her goals.

"I could never have imagined the response to this experiment from both friends and strangers alike," she says. "I experienced moments of pure connection with people, connection on a level where we can all agree that life is a blessing and that we have much to be grateful for. Beyond all our differences, there is gratitude."

Along the way, Jo-Anne learned a lot about the power of gratefulness to transform lives. Here she recounts some of the most significant:

I have learned that I can step way outside my comfort zone, and live to tell the tale.

I have learned that I can ask for help, and that my courage grows in the asking.

I have learned that "What are you grateful for?" is the best conversation starter ever.

I have learned that gratitude is a lens that is always within my grasp.

I have learned that there are others who are dedicating themselves to celebrating gratitude, and I will continue to turn to them for inspiration in those moments when gratitude does not come easily.

Jo-Anne's next plan is to run her first New York City

marathon, in November 2014. "Inspired by so many of the people I met this past year, I plan to use this new 'project' as a platform to raise awareness and funds for charitable causes within my community," she says.

GRATEFUL LIFE PRACTICE: GRATITUDE AS A SPIRITUAL LENS

I use gratitude as a spiritual lens. It's very easy to pick up when all is right with the world. But I make an intentional effort to view those situations that challenge me through this same lens. I ask myself, "What would this situation look like through the lens of gratitude?" This is a question I use whenever I need to. It was a very powerful tool that I used last April, for example, as I experienced the death of a beloved aunt. It transformed an incredibly sad and painful time into a spiritually rich time that I shall never forget.

Create a Joy Jar

I keep a jar, a pen, and pieces of paper in a visible and easily accessible place in my home. Whenever I experience something joyful—a moment, a conversation, an experience, an insight, or an encounter—I write it down and stick it in the Joy Jar. Then, at the end of the year, I review it and remember those moments.

As 2014 began, Jo-Anne wrote, "The Joy Jar is now empty and ready to receive my joyful moments for 2014."

GETTING TO THE SOUL OF
GRATITUDE PRACTICE

I don't have to chase extraordinary moments to find happiness. It's right in front of me if I'm paying attention and practicing gratitude.

—Brene Brown

In 1989, Susanne West's daughter Heidi, then 18, was diagnosed with a progressively debilitative and degenerative form of arthritis and Crohn's disease.

During that difficult year, when Heidi was told that this disease, Ankylosing Spondylitis, and Crohn's disease progressively eat at her spine and sacroiliac joints, eventually causing fusion of the spine, Susanne, a professor of psychology at John F. Kennedy University in California, became a primary caregiver for her daughter.

"I was obsessed with doing everything humanly possible on all practical fronts and with providing

emotional and moral support for Heidi as well," she says. When she had any free time, Susanne felt guilty that she wasn't doing more. "I felt I should be investigating treatments, or looking for books or tapes she'd enjoy.

"Throughout, I was highly stressed because of the severity of her symptoms, the pain she was experiencing, and the complications around finding the right treatments and practitioners. Getting entangled in the health care maze and dealing with insurance was another huge stressor."

Fast-forward more than 20 years. Heidi was diagnosed with breast cancer in the fifth month of her pregnancy. Susanne dove into the deep sea of full-time caregiving again. Caregiving included going with her to chemo treatments, watching the new baby during the treatments, being available to Heidi post-chemo, spending more time with the other children, purchasing items she needed, working with others to organize the house, make schedules, etc., and helping her navigate issues with insurance, doctors, and medications.

"I knew by then that self-care had to be a priority for me if I was to serve her and her children in the healthiest ways possible," she says.

That is where gratitude stepped in. Instead of stressing out, as she knows she did the first time her daughter was ill, Susanne had developed a tool kit for self-care. It was time to draw from its bank again.

"After the initial shock, and fully facing a wide range of feelings, I found myself grateful that I had come to understand and practice so much about self-care," she remembers. "My caregiving during that time was based on Heidi's needs as defined by her and her husband, always making sure that I balanced my own needs with hers and the children's." She chronicles her gratefulness and journey to the soul in her book, Soul Care for Caregivers: How to Help Yourself While Helping Others.

Susanne says that she grew more spiritually as a result of Heidi's illnesses than she did from over 25 years of spiritual practice. She is deeply grateful for the qualities that she inadvertently developed over the years: "presence, empathy, courage, strength, acceptance, resilience, generosity, trust, mindfulness, and compassion."

"Is it possible, I wonder, that her diseases really are blessings in my life, catalyzing transformation in ways I never could have imagined?" she asks herself. "I see that just about everything about me has changed over the last few years—my understanding of what's really important in life, beliefs about who I am and what I can and cannot do, old patterns, illusions, coping strategies, ways of being in the world and with others, and beliefs about health and healing, life, death, and suffering. The other important insight, which is why I wrote the book, is that, because caregiving can be very stressful in many different ways, self-care is imperative.

"I am deeply grateful that I have learned how to very fully 'show up' for my daughter and her family, and not lose myself in the process," Susanne says. "I understand the value of self-care now from my head to my toes. And these lessons about self-care that I have learned as a caregiver for my daughter (and over the last two years with my 87-year-old mother) have spilled over into every area of my life. I take self-care breaks of all sorts, no matter what I'm involved with, and everything that needs to get done, gets done—a lot more easefully than ever before."

To access her inner wisdom, Susanne employs writing and self-guided imagery practices, which she says she "uses all the time, especially when I am 'stretched' " with regard to caregiving. Here, she shares a self-guided imagery practice for tapping into thankfulness and relieving stress.

GRATEFUL LIFE PRACTICE: MEDITATION

Bring to mind a time when you felt very grateful. You may have received good news about a friend or family member, or perhaps you were surprised by a wonderful gift from someone you care about.

Relive that experience as if it's happening now.

Notice feelings and physical sensations as you vividly recall this experience of gratitude. Experience this from your head to your toes for two to four minutes, or as long as you would like.

Then let go of this particular memory, but continue to relax into the positive sensations that feeling grateful evokes in you.

At various points throughout the day, take a minute or two to bring this experience into your awareness.

On another day you may choose to recall a different memory of gratitude.

You will likely have many bright moments on the days that you do this practice.

ON THAT NOTE:
WRITE A THANK-YOU CARD

E-mail is great for many things—thanking people is not one of them.

Stumped on when to write it out versus type it? Consider a handwritten note after:

- Formal parties. Beyond thanking the host when you leave, follow up with a second sign of gratitude. Never underestimate the power of a written note sent via snail mail—it's always appreciated, under any circumstances.
- Weddings and showers. Write the notes and get them out ASAP, but always within three months of the actual event. A little more leeway is allowed here, keeping in mind the chaos of these big events.
- Receiving congratulatory (or condolence) gifts.

Lesson Plan
The general rule of thumb is getting your thank-you notes out within a month; if you miss that deadline, start the

letter with something like, "I've been meaning to reach out and thank you for..."

1. Start with a salutation. For example, write "Dear Grandpa," or "To My Aunt Diane." Remember to triple-check the spelling if using a proper name—the idea is to appear thoughtful, not the opposite.

2. Express your gratitude. You can start with "Thank you for..." Never directly mention cash; instead, refer to monetary gifts as "your generosity" or "your thoughtfulness." Don't forget to mention your gratitude for non-tangible gifts as well: "Thank you for attending Christmas Eve dinner," etc.

3. Include specific details to show your appreciation. Tell the person how you plan to use the gift, or how it has already come in handy: "I can't wait to use the bag on my next trip abroad." You should come off as happy and grateful, but not insincere, so try not to lie, even if you don't like the gift. If the gift was a gesture rather than a physical thing, thank them for taking the time, or for their thoughtfulness. If the gift was money, hint around what you might spend it on, but don't call out specific items—naming items may cause the giver to feel bad about not knowing what you wanted.

4. Add a personal sentiment. "I look forward to seeing you over Easter" or "I hope to see you soon" both signal a real relationship outside of the confines of gift-giving and letter-writing.

5. Restate your thanks. Drive home your gratitude, but in a different way, giving one more example of thanks: "Again, thank you for your generosity. I'm so excited about my upcoming trip to…"

6. End with a warm closing followed by your signature. Depending on what feels natural to you, "With love," "Warmly," "Best," or "Cheers," are all solid options, followed by a comma, then add your signature on the next line.

Source: Thank you to The Old School, www.theoldschool.com, an online media site dedicated to bringing inspiration, education, and sharing to the vast "hands-on" audience—all the foodies, crafters, DIYers, and urban homesteaders out there.

HELPING HAND:
BLESSING BAGS FOR THE HOMELESS

Like many of us, Rachael Crawford always felt torn when she would find herself at a traffic light in downtown Baltimore next to a homeless man or woman standing on the corner, or when she would be walking past them on the street. She felt compelled to help, wished there was something to do, but felt uncomfortable about handing them money, then guilty if she did nothing.

That's when the 22-year-old Carroll County, Maryland, resident saw an idea on Pinterest for "Blessing Bags," plastic bags filled with toiletries and non-perishable goods that you can keep in your car or purse to hand out to the homeless.

It sounds like a simple idea, and it is one that is

working its way across the Internet, inspiring people across the country to give back and help those less blessed than themselves.

Rachael, who works during the week as a private daycare provider and weekends pursuing a career as a rodeo rider (yes, she rides bulls), has been recovering from a bad fall in September during a rodeo in Pennsylvania. "I got stomped on and shattered my shoulder as well as fractured my spine in three places," she says. Since then, she has had two surgeries, is in intensive physical therapy, and was unable to work for five months.

Instead of feeling sorry for herself, she decided to do something to help others. That is when she created the Blessing Bags.

"Despite being hurt, I've been in plenty worse situations and know there are people out there who would give anything to be in my shoes," she says.

Since she launched a Facebook page, "Blessing Bags," to inspire others, the project has taken on a special significance. She spent the months of December 2013 and January 2014 distributing the bags to the homeless in Baltimore.

On her Facebook page she writes: "My name is Rachael and I created this page to provide people with a unique way of helping those in need. I myself have been through a very dark period of my life where I was homeless, living on the streets and in abandoned houses, going days without eating, being so cold that I couldn't sleep despite how exhausted I was, I was feeling like nothing would ever get better and that nobody cared. Now that I have been so blessed and turned my life around I do everything I can to help those in need. When you have been there yourself, you understand those in need that much more."

She says when she passes someone on the street, "or when they come up to my car begging for money, there is a hesitation to help because of the fear they will put the money towards drugs or getting high. I can assure you from personal experience that is true. The Blessing Bags are a better way to assure yourself they will go towards making someone's day better in a healthy way and not contributing to unhealthy habits."

She says, "Bull riding saved my life, it got me clean and off the streets, and I now have healthy relationships with all of my family members, and an entire new outlook on life. I want to help others."

How you can help: Blessing Bags include everyday essentials from hairbrushes and toothpaste to playing cards, gloves, snacks, and other non-perishable items. You keep them handy, and when you encounter someone in need, hand them a Blessing Bag.

But Rachael's bags have another twist. Each includes an inspirational Bible passage. "When these bags are given to someone in need, it shows you noticed them and cared despite how lonely they feel. It gives them hope."

HONORING THE SIMPLE MOMENTS
OF GRATITUDE

*So much has been given to me; I have no time to
ponder over that which has been denied.*

—Helen Keller

*Everyone has a gratitude story. Here are some transcripts
of recent conversations with people just like you!*

IN SERVING OTHERS

"My Christmas and New Year vacation cruise was a time
of true reflection. My intention is to answer my calling of
giving service, which for me is gratitude in action. In early
January of 2014, I went to West Africa to do service in my
capacity as a Rotarian."

    —Dr. Cynthia Barnett, Retirement Life Coach Founder
and CEO of Retirement Academy, Norwalk, Connecticut

THE KINDNESS OF OTHERS

"When I was in physical rehab after my broken leg and second hip surgery, some of the most unlikely people thought of me or came to visit. One colleague brought his young kids a couple of times. They were just what the place needed, and they entertained the others, who were much older and more 'sick' than I was. Another colleague and his wife stopped by, just to say hi. A friend and colleague who was on assignment in New Jersey drove up and gave me a funny elf statue to keep me company. Another one brought her dog to the nursing home to visit, and she and my friend Julie caught me as I was walking, for the first time, down the hall with a walker. Lots of celebrating (including the dog). One of my mom's doctors sent me roses. Even the cards I got that found their way even though they were misaddressed reminded me that this too shall pass."

—Elida Witthoeft, Senior Coordinating Producer
for ESPN, Bristol, Connecticut

THE HEAT IS ON

Every morning, Monica Dougherty, a Chicago art therapist and author, sends out "grateful messages for the amazingly efficient heater in my office, as I want to keep working through this season." She adds, "Everywhere I look, little things are falling apart, and it seems overwhelming until I remember that this is how life works. Things fall apart, batteries need replacement, tires get flat, cars get older and are subject to more problems, garage door openers act crazy (ours flips out every couple of months!), and everyone has these issues at times. I am trying to stay positive and remember that it's not my knees or hips that need replacing, only batteries, and at least I have a garage during this brutal winter. It's just one foot in front of the other until things improve. That's the one big message I keep in mind from a book I received—that just by reaching for the better feeling (even if it's minute) the energy shifts."

ALL IN THE FAMILY

Family is at the top of his list of blessings for Jay Schenk of St. Charles, Missouri. He says he finds gratitude in every day through "the miracle of life, and especially the life of grandkids. Carter was born with a complete cleft and other complications, and we almost lost him on his second day of life. After all the surgeries, seven years later, what an amazing and free spirit he is!

"Another grandson, Michael Patrick, was born with a tumor on his vocal cord. It wasn't cancer, but the doctors said it would come back. After three months, they checked him again, and it was back and bigger. So once again they were going to remove another portion of it. My wife, Mary, and I were at Holy Family parish the night before the surgery. Bishop Sartain of Joliet sat with us for dinner, and we told him about Michael. He said that there is a shrine at Holy Family and, when we were done, we should go and pray together. So we did. When he left he said he would also be praying for Michael when he said Mass the next morning. Chuck Neff, a friend of ours who was hosting a radio show on Relevant Radio, did a show of prayer for Michael. We were driving back to St. Louis (from Chicago) and got word that, when they went in to remove that portion of the tumor, not only could they not find it, they didn't even see scar tissue from the first surgery."

And of course, Jay adds, "My wife of 40 years is an angel to all, with countless gifts of caring for others. We have four beautiful daughters who have given us seven grandchildren; they all lead lives of faith and are always helping each other or others."

IN LIVING COLOR

"It was only a year ago that my friends and I decided to try an evening of painting at an event where you create artwork in a 'fun and relaxing environment.' I was more interested in the wine, snacks, and laughing with my group, but I discovered that evening that I truly love to paint. Since then, I have signed up for lessons in oil painting and drawing. While I have a long way to go, I have found joy not only in painting but in sharing my work with family and friends. I believe there is a 'waiting artist' in all of us!"

—Helene Gillespie, Palatine, Illinois

WITH STRINGS ATTACHED: WEAR YOUR GRATITUDE WITH A BLESSING BRACELET

Every single day do something that makes your heart sing.

—Marcia Wieder

Dawn Sprong wears her gratitude on her sleeve. Literally. A couple of years ago, the founder of MAI Apparel (Made As Intended) attached a message to be grateful to her close circle of friends on the signature bracelets she made for holiday gifts and special occasions. She says she created the bracelets because she had experienced "a profound shift in my own life and thinking."

"I had this constant nagging feeling that my life seemed pointless," Dawn remembers. "I kept asking myself, 'What is the point of all this?'"

At the time, Dawn had a highly successful career in

the sports industry. But that wasn't enough, so she left to have children and launch her own business in the hopes it would provide the flexibility she was seeking.

"I left sports 18 years ago when I adopted my children," she says. "I changed to working with kids and families mainly to satisfy my feeling of life not feeling very deep or profound. At first I did feel I was making a difference in my new company, but the feeling of pointlessness returned. Truly the only thing that saved me was realizing my thinking and actions had to change to truly change everything."

She had the nice car and the beautiful home, and lived to "live up to my neighbors' standards," she says. "I was struggling with some major life changes, and it came to me that life was a struggle in part because, no matter what I had or what I asked for, it was never enough. I never slowed down enough to sit in appreciation. I was getting everything I was asking for, but I wasn't asking for the things that really matter."

She started taking notice of the blessings in her life, and her life changed. She withdrew from the rat race, left an unhealthy marriage, examined her life, left behind "an obsession with money and getting ahead," and went in search of what is possible.

"Suddenly the world looked brighter, and I realized that being grateful was truly a way to live," she says. "It was also giving me a doorway into being able to truly *open my heart to the world and make the difference I had always thought possible."*

Fast forward to three years ago. That is when she took the bracelets she'd been making for her girlfriends and officially created Blessing Bracelets. Within a week, she had orders for 20 bracelets—after two weeks, 50. The rest is history. Since 2011, Made As Intended has shipped over 300,000 Blessing Bracelets to more than 1,000 retailers across the globe, from the United States to England to Canada and Italy. The bracelets have given birth to a global gratitude movement, she says.

Dawn receives letters daily from across the world thanking her for the Blessing Bracelets. They come from people who lost a loved one to cancer and wear the bracelets in honor of their memory. Others are from mothers who give them to their daughters, thanking them for the gifts their lives have been. One man wrote to say he buried his wife with a bracelet because she was the kind of person who appreciated everything in her life and he wanted her to carry that gratefulness into the afterlife.

"The whole idea is so that people can move gratitude from their subconscious to the place where they can be in awe for the blessings in their life," Dawn says.

Blessing Bracelets are extremely personal bracelets that can tell the gratitude story of your life. Made from sterling silver and Swarovski pearls or gemstones, these one-size-fits-all bracelets are designed so that when you wear one, you are acknowledging one blessing in your life for each of the bracelet's four pearls. Each time you are drawn to the bracelet, the intention is to silently find four people or things in your life you can be grateful for.

Here's some inspiration: Be grateful for your children, a flower, your dog, a perfect cup of coffee, and a roof over your head—just something.

The idea is simple: The more you wear the Blessing Bracelets, the more blessings you find, the more you will be blessed. In one year, you will be aware of a profound change in your life, says Dawn.

Today, Dawn is remarried, and she and her husband and their collective four teenagers (he has two, she has two), along with nine full-time workers, handcraft the bracelets in the living room of their suburban Chicago home, shipping them from their dining room table.

Part of the company's mission is to "inspire human-kind to make a spirit-based shift of perspective," she says. She thought the apparel would be the low-hanging fruit, but these days it is the Blessing Bracelets that are driving company revenue.

Dawn practices what she preaches. She and her family "lead a very eclectic life" that welcomes people and animals who are hurting to their home. There is a family they've welcomed who are regular guests, and they've adopted four shelter dogs, two donkeys, a couple of chickens, and three birds. "We've been very blessed and want our home to be a spiritual community that embraces all," Dawn says. Her dream is "to build and live in a community that is welcoming to all."

MAI (Made As Intended) is a conscious company and community of "like-minded people following the message of our hearts," she says. "We have a purpose, inspiring others to follow their hearts, find their dreams, and create the world as they wish to see it. As a conscious company, we hope to reflect that every choice we make affects others, from the products we buy to the prices we set. We do not propose telling anyone else what to do; we are conscious of what we do."

Each blessing bracelet comes with a beautiful reminder that the purpose of the bracelet is to increase gratitude worldwide.

GRATEFUL LIFE PRACTICE: THREE TIPS FOR PRACTICING GRATEFULNESS ON "BAD DAYS"

Some days are hard. It seems as if everything is going wrong. So how are you supposed to tap into your gratefulness? Dawn offers three ways to feel better and be grateful:

1. Be thankful for honesty. When you're just not feeling gratitude, she suggests you should be grateful for being honest about that.

2. Be thankful for awareness. Be grateful that you even

thought about not feeling grateful. That means gratefulness is part of your daily experience and part of your consciousness.

3. Build it and they will come. The fact that you are struggling to find what you are grateful for helps you see for yourself that there is always something to be grateful for. Sometimes you have to say thank you "just because" and wait for the blessing to manifest itself. Something will always surface if you have the intention to be grateful every day. It will help you to see not only what there is in the world around you, but what is inside of you, says Dawn.

HOW TO BRING MORE GRATITUDE
INTO YOUR LIFE

Be grateful. Sounds obvious but we bring more gratitude into our lives by being grateful. Wherever gratitude goes, gratitude grows.

Desire to be grateful. It requires no special skill or talent, simply a genuine desire to open our hearts and be willing to change our perspective.

Share it. "If I look to my experience over the past year especially, my gratitude grew by sharing it with others, by connecting with others. It is one thing to be grateful in the silence of our own hearts, but gratitude takes on a whole new dimension when I give it a voice."

Serve others. Put it into action by loving and serving others, and you will get past the fear of what others may think of you and dare to be grateful.

ACKNOWLEDGMENTS

Mary Beth is thankful for:

My friend Jenny, who on the hardest days during my mom's hospitalization and illness, would drop notes of support in my mailbox.

Writing opportunities born out of everyday living—care giving and spiritual healing.

Little Tommy, my grandson, born months after losing my mom.

Challenging business experiences that reinforced my belief that it is important to do unto others, personally and professionally, and have given me the opportunity to forgive and move on.

The "Book Ladies" and my circle of friends. They're too long to list, too special to not be extremely grateful for.

My neighbor, who after my sixth round of snow-shoveling duties during a particularly snowy day in January of 2014, came over with his snow blower to plow the impacted snow at the bottom of my driveway.

The hospital angels Tricia and Robert, who hovered with compassion and care during the last six years.

My Caribou Coffee friends, I appreciate your smiles and encouragement and the pick-me-up every morning before heading to the hospital.

Dr. Leasak, for your honesty in telling me what I had to do during my mother's illness.

My daughters, for helping me know I dress cool by borrowing my clothes.

My son and Ginia, for bringing Rylee and little Tommy into this world.

For my dogs who "walk me" at a brisk 12 mile-a-minute pace.

Nina is thankful for:

Martin Eggenberger, the most steadfast and skilled skipper both on the high seas and on land.

The waters in and around the San Francisco Bay for keeping our sailboat *Gratitude* afloat. For the sea lions and dolphins who swim alongside her in those waters. For the wind and currents that carry her to new places to explore.

My children, Mara and Jaime, for being their own persons. I deeply appreciate your humor, love, and values.

My dog Biscuit and cat Cookie who keep me company and entertain me daily.

Viva Editions, which earned the designation "Publisher of the Year," in 2014. Brenda Knight, you are publisher of the century in my book!

The staff of The Greater Good Science Center in Berkeley, California for their focus on positive change.

My garden for providing "local" and organic produce.

Friendships. I am so grateful to all of you.

Litquake, San Francisco's literary festival.

Life itself. For living in a beautiful area and for my health.

ABOUT THE AUTHORS

 NINA LESOWITZ is an award-winning marketing professional who runs Spinergy Group, which represents authors, corporate clients, and nonprofits. She, along with Sammons, coauthored the bestselling *Living Life as a Thank You* and *What Would You Do if You Knew You Could Not Fail?: How to Transform Fear into Courage.* She lives and sails in the San Francisco Bay Area with her husband, and produces events for Litquake, San Francisco's literary festival.

MARY BETH SAMMONS is a "gratitude entrepreneur" who creates new reasons each day to be thankful. She's an award-winning journalist and author of eight books about making a difference, including *Second Acts That Change Lives: Making a Difference in the World* (Conari Press) and *We Carry Each Other: Getting Through Life's Toughest Times*. Mary Beth has carved out a career in helping surface stories of "ordinary people doing extraordinary things," and is a frequent contributor to the *Chicago Tribune*, Beliefnet.com, and EldercareAbc.com. A cause-related marketing specialist, she helps foundations and nonprofit organizations surface their compelling stories and spread the good news. She lives with her three children in Chicago's north suburbs.